"The quotations contained in The Genius of Robert E. Lee, brings this great commander to life. Al Kaltman masterfully presents Lee's personality, warlike virtues and human frailties. Lee's leadership style and techniques are as relevant today as they were at Chancellorsville. Great leaders inspire us to greater efforts, whether on the modern battlefield or in business."

Donald R. Gardner
Major General, USMC (Ret.)
CEO, Marine Corps University Foundation
The Robert A. Lutz Distinguished Chair of Military Studies,
  Marine Corps University

"I personally witnessed Al Kaltman apply his management principles to successfully re-engineer our company, establishing a firm foundation for us to build on. Now he shares some of that same wisdom in his brilliant portrayal of the leadership of Robert E. Lee."

Timothy D. Bruns
Acting President and CEO
Merastar Insurance Company

"Robert E. Lee exercised leadership in circumstances that yielded dramatic triumphs as well as shattering failures. This book successfully probes his career in search of lessons that contemporary leaders, both civilian and military, can apply to a range of questions and problems."

Gary W. Gallagher
University of Virginia
John L. Nau III Professor in the History of the American Civil War
Author of *Lee and His Generals in War and Memory*, *The Confederate War*, and other works.

"If you are in the business of directing, managing, or leading people to higher performance or if you just like history, then you need to read this book. Dr. Kaltman knows that nothing is more potent than a good example, and Robert E. Lee is a good example of an exemplary leader with character."

Dr. J. Rodney Short
Professor, Educational Leadership and Former Associate Dean
Texas Woman's University
Recipient of the Distinguished Mentor Award from the
University of Texas Superintendent's Academy

"Kaltman finds the mother lode of Lee's practical genius and spiritual greatness. From this, he mines lessons of leadership that are marvelously modern and thoroughly accessible to anyone who needs to leverage limited resources to the utmost and inspire people to achieve beyond all expectation. The Genius of Robert E. Lee is a unique set of guideposts for today's ambitious entrepreneur: the underdog who means to settle for nothing less than victory."

Alan Axelrod
Author of *Patton on Leadership: Strategic Lessons for Corporate Warfare and Elizabeth I, CEO: Strategic Lessons from the Leader Who Built an Empire*

"Readers of this fascinating book will absorb many practical lessons of leadership from America's most revered general. They will also peer into some of the most alluring moments of Lee's life and of the Civil War. It offers an inspiring treat for leaders, managers in the making, and history buffs alike."

David J. Eicher
Author of *Robert E. Lee: A Life Portrait,*
The Civil War in Books, and other works.

"As a novelist, I can only dream of coming up with a character as rich as Robert E. Lee. Al Kaltman extracts General Lee's unique blend of common sense, humanity, and leadership, and distills it into hard-hitting lessons for managers—perfect execution of a terrific idea."

Terry Baxter
President, White Mountains Holdings, and author of
Hailstone and *The Ursa Ultimatum.*

"The author traces Lee's activities and military decisions both before and during the Civil War; from these he infers maxims that are useful in life generally. An insightful and clever use of historical data."

Alan T. Nolan
Author of *Lee Considered*

"This book should be on every manager's bookshelf. It uses excellent examples to demonstrate the basic tenets of management. Each piece of advice is a reminder of what managers should be doing

A. Thomas Hollingsworth
Dean, School of Business, Florida Institute of Technology

"Al Kaltman makes you think about changing titles used in business—General or President . . . is there a difference? After reading this excellent book, it is clear that leadership is leadership whether it's running a country, army, or corporation. The book reaffirms and supports leadership traits."

Thomas W. Crawford
President, Retail Distribution
Sr. Vice President, The Prudential Insurance Company of America

It is history that teaches us to hope.

—Robert E. Lee

All the quotations are by Robert E. Lee, unless otherwise noted.

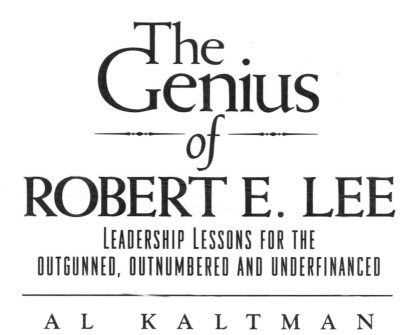

The Genius
of
ROBERT E. LEE

Leadership Lessons for the
Outgunned, Outnumbered and Underfinanced

A L K A L T M A N

Prentice
Hall Press

Library of Congress Cataloging-in-Publication Data

Kaltman, Al.
   The genius of Robert E. Lee : leadership lessons for the
outgunned, outmanned, and underfinanced / [Al Kaltman].
      p. cm.
   Includes index.
   ISBN 0-7352-0187-0
   1. Lee, Robert E. (Robert Edward), 1807–1870—Military
leadership. 2. Lee, Robert E. (Robert Edward), 1807–1870—
Quotations. 3. Generals—Confederate States of America—
Biography. 4. Command of troops. 5. Leadership—Case studies.
6. Management—United States—Case studies. 7. United States—
History—Civil War, 1861–1865—Campaigns. I. Title.

E467.1.L4 K35 2001
973.7'3'092—dc21   00–062370

Acquisitions Editor: *Tom Power*
Production Editor: *Eve Mossman*
Interior Design/Layout: *Dee Coroneos*

Printed in the United States of America

10 9 8 7 6 5 4 3 2 1

ISBN 0-7352-0187-0

 Paramus, NJ 07652

http://www.phdirect.com

To

Mylan and Blaine
who, like Custis, Rooney and Rob,
received more than their fair share
of fatherly advice.

ACKNOWLEDGMENTS

I couldn't have been more than twelve years old, when one day, while browsing in the library, I picked up a copy of Douglas Southall Freeman's *Lee's Lieutenants*. Enthralled, I sat down in the aisle between the book stacks and began to read. Years later, I renewed my acquaintance with Freeman when I read his monumental four-volume biography of the South's greatest leader. All of us who have studied the life of Robert E. Lee are forever in Freeman's debt.

I am also indebted to Lee's other biographers, especially Burke Davis, David J. Eicher, Alan T. Nolan, Margaret Sanborn and Emory M. Thomas, and to many Civil War historians, particularly Bevin Alexander, William C. Davis, Shelby Foote, Gary W. Gallagher, James M. McPherson and Steven E. Woodworth.

My wife, Gwen, deserves a large measure of the credit for this book. She critiqued every page as it came off the printer, and then edited and re-edited the manuscript until she was convinced it represented my best efforts.

To Ed Knappman and Tom Power, who believed in this book, I am deeply grateful. Colonel Charles Goode, USMC (ret.), Liz Hatch, Kim Holien, Joe and Myra Rakosky, Rodney Short and John Simon reviewed an early draft, correcting inaccuracies and offering suggestions for improvement. Patrick Byrne performed the difficult task of reviewing what I thought was the final copy of the manuscript. His editorial comments and corrections were invaluable. I also received assistance from staff members at the

Library of Congress, Marine Corps University Foundation, National Archives, National Museum of the American Indian, United States Military Academy, Valentine Museum, Virginia Historical Society and Washington and Lee University.

The "marble man" image of Robert E. Lee is so ingrained and intimidating that I approached the writing of this book with trepidation. To my relief, I found Lee human, witty and wise. It has been a joy to follow in his footsteps.

CONTENTS

PREFACE

Robert E. Lee is an American icon. After Washington and Lincoln, he is our most respected and admired historical figure. Traditional high school and college textbooks treat him almost reverentially. There is a building named in his honor on the campus of the United States Military Academy at West Point, and a seemingly countless number of roads and schools bear his name. Washington founded a great nation; Lincoln preserved it. Lee led an army in a revolution whose purpose was the dissolution of the United States of America. For a military leader of a failed revolt to be held in such universal esteem is unprecedented in all of human history and represents a remarkable and continuing tribute to a great leader.

This book presents incidents from the life of Robert E. Lee. For each I have provided modern management advice that can be applied by today's civilian and military leaders. The incidents are presented chronologically rather than grouped by management topics. Lee, like anyone who has been privileged to lead others, learned his leadership lessons in the context of his experiences. He didn't set out one day to learn all he would ever need to know about communication, delegation, or any other subject. To take what we can learn from him out of historical context leaves us with a disembodied list of principles and deprives us of the opportunity to get to know one of America's greatest leaders.

Lee lived a fascinating life. Graduated second in his class at West Point, he did important work for the Army Corps of Engineers. He received three promotions and numerous commendations for his performance during the Mexican War, was superintendent of West Point, commanded cavalry on the Texas frontier, managed a Virginia plantation, and was the Confederacy's leading general. After the Civil War, he was a role model for the defeated South, and as president of Washington

College (now Washington and Lee University), he laid the foundation for a great educational institution.

Field Marshal Viscount (Garnet J.) Wolseley, when he was a lieutenant colonel, served for a time with Lee's army as a British observer. He felt that Lee was "one of the few men that ever seriously impressed and awed me with their natural, their inherent greatness."

I shall never forget his sweet, winning smile, nor his clear honest eyes that seemed to look into your heart while they searched your brain. . . . He is stamped upon my memory as being apart and superior to all others in every way, a man with whom none I ever knew and few of whom I have ever read are worthy to be classed.

Robert E. Lee was a great leader who exemplified our most admirable virtues. But he was not perfect. If he had been, there would be no point in writing a book of leadership advice drawn from his life's story. Perfection is too high a bar. With all his sterling qualities, Lee was subject to common human frailties. His mistakes are the basis for some of the most valuable lessons we can learn. Lee was too wise to look for perfection in himself or others. What he sought was constant improvement. He believed:

The education of a man or woman is never complete till they die. There is always before them much to learn and more to do. Our hardest lesson is self-knowledge, and it is one that is perhaps never accomplished.

Lee never wrote his memoirs, but from his correspondence and reminiscences of his friends and family, I have been able to include a quotation by him with most of the incidents described in this book. His words are sometimes entertaining. They are invariably clear, concise and forceful. Fortunately for us, he never broke what he called his "old habit of giving advice," because today's leaders will find Robert E. Lee's advice invaluable.

1

PULL OUT ALL
THE STOPS

January 1807–August 1837

The son of a Revolutionary War hero, Robert E. Lee uses every means at his disposal to secure an appointment to West Point. Graduated second in his class, he begins his career as an engineering officer. His early assignments expose Lee to the difficulties associated with serving in a peacetime army.

1. STICK TO YOUR KNITTING

*R*OBERT EDWARD LEE'S FATHER WAS THE FAMOUS Revolutionary War hero Henry Lee, better known as Light Horse Harry. In 1782, he resigned from the army. In a letter to his commanding officer, General Nathanael Greene, he wrote, "I wish from motives of self to make my way easy and comfortable." When he received the letter of resignation, General Greene remarked that, while Henry Lee could resign from the army, he couldn't "cease to be a soldier."

After leaving the army, Henry Lee engaged in a series of ruinous business ventures that left him destitute. In 1809, when Robert was two, his father spent nearly a year in jail for failing to pay his debts. Four years later, to escape his creditors, he sailed for Barbados in the West Indies. Robert never saw his father again.

ADVICE

If you find something you are good at and enjoy doing, stick with it. Do not be tempted into some other field simply because you think you can make more money. You have to be able to support yourself, but you also need to feel good about what you do for a living. You will perform better at a job you have a passion for, and rewards follow performance.

*A*NOTHER REASON FOR HENRY LEE'S LEAVING THE army was that he had not been promoted. He came to feel that his services were not adequately appreciated by his friends and were denigrated by his enemies. He wrote that because of "the persecution of my foes" he saw no alternative but to resign from the army. General Greene tried to get him to change his mind.

I wish you would not think of leaving the service. Everybody knows I have the highest opinion of you as an officer. . . . I believe few officers in America or Europe are held in higher estimation.

A D V I C E

When things don't go your way, you aren't promoted, or the assignment you wanted is given to someone else, it is all too easy to start imagining that there are people who are out to get you. There may be times when it is appropriate for you to resign your position and seek another outlet for your talents, but succumbing to the belief that you are the victim of a conspiracy will lead you to make bad career choices.

3. BAD MOUTHING

*H*ENRY LEE'S FINANCIAL DIFFICULTIES MADE HIM AN object of ridicule. Some of his neighbors delighted in spreading malicious gossip about him. They told the story of the time he asked to borrow a horse from a neighbor. The man agreed to let him do so, but, wanting to be sure he would get his horse back, he had one of his slaves accompany General Lee on a second horse with instructions to bring back the borrowed horse. It was some weeks later before the slave returned. He told his owner that he had been unable to bring back the horses because Henry Lee had sold them. When asked why he hadn't then immediately returned home, he replied, "'Cause General Lee sold me, too."

ADVICE

Some people delight in other's misfortunes. When someone is having difficulties at work, peers can act like sharks in a feeding frenzy, only too anxious to spread the most outrageous gossip about the troubled co-worker. Don't allow yourself to be drawn into gossip mongering, and don't countenance it among your staff.

4. PULL OUT ALL THE STOPS

*A*T THE AGE OF SEVENTEEN, ROBERT E. LEE DECIDED to apply for admission to the United States Military Academy at West Point. To gain admittance, Lee mounted his first campaign. He began by securing an interview with the Secretary of War, John C. Calhoun of South Carolina, a state that his father had helped to liberate from the British. At that interview, Lee presented the Secretary with a letter of introduction from a family friend who knew Calhoun. He followed up with letters of recommendation from his teacher and two of his older brothers. He also wrote a letter on his own behalf, and he obtained a letter from his Congressman.

Lee's Congressman, along with two other Congressmen and five United States Senators, signed the following letter to Secretary Calhoun:

We beg leave to recommend to your favorable consideration Mr. Robert Edward Lee, a son of the late General Henry Lee of Virginia, as an applicant for admission to the Military Academy at West Point.

The assurances which we have received of the talents and attainments of this young gentleman, apart from the regard we feel for the military services of his deceased father, induce us to hope that the gratification of his wishes may prove compatible with the rules which you have deemed it proper to establish for the admission of cadets into the Academy.

A D V I C E

When hiring, ask yourself how much does the applicant really want the job. Was the application letter perfect? Were all supporting documents complete? Were extra materials, e.g., writing samples, provided without being asked? How much of an effort was made to learn about your organization? The people you want to hire are the ones that want the job so badly they develop a plan to get it, and then use every favorable advantage they have to help secure it, leaving nothing to chance or happenstance.

5. BE OVERPREPARED

*L*EE WAS APPOINTED TO WEST POINT IN MARCH 1824. Since that year's class was already filled, he had to wait until the July 1825 class before he could begin his studies. A major portion of the curriculum at West Point was devoted to mathematics. While waiting for his class to start, he went to a school in Alexandria, Virginia. His teacher, Benjamin Hallowell, had this to say of Lee's pre-West Point studies:

His specialty was finishing up. He imparted a finish and a neatness, as he proceeded to everything he undertook. One of the branches of mathematics he studied with me was Conic Sections, in which some of the diagrams are very complicated. He drew the diagrams on a slate; and although he well knew that the one he was drawing would have to be removed to make room for another, he drew each one with as much accuracy and finish, lettering and all, as if it were to be engraved and printed.

As a result of his preparatory studies, Lee had already covered the subject matter taught during the first year of mathematics at the Academy. This gave him a considerable leg-up as he could devote extra time to studying French, the only other academic subject taught that year. Lee finished the year ranked third in his class and was appointed a cadet staff sergeant, the highest position to which someone finishing his plebe year could be promoted.

A D V I C E

There is no such thing as being too prepared. Use the time prior to the start of an assignment to get as ready as possible. When considering someone for an assignment, ask yourself how much effort that person put into getting ready for his or her last project.

6. YOU CAN'T ALWAYS BE #1

*L*EE'S NEMESIS AT WEST POINT WAS A CADET FROM New York, Charles Mason. In each of their first three years at the Academy, Mason ranked first in the class. Lee was ranked third in their first year and second in each of the next two years.

In their final year, Lee worked hard to beat Mason. He even paid to be tutored in mineralogy. Lee also received permission to move to a nearby hotel for the two months prior to the final examinations. There he was able to study without distraction.

Lee gave it his very best, but his best was not good enough. Charles Mason still graduated first in their class. Lee came in second.

ADVICE

Even star performers occasionally come in second. Highly competitive people are generally able to deal with work-place disappointments such as not getting the top bonus. As a manager, you want to have overachievers working for you, but be leery of those who cannot cope if they're not always number one.

After graduating, Charles Mason taught engineering at West Point before resigning from the army to study law. He never again served in the military.

7. TO RISE FROM THE RANKS

*E*VEN THOUGH CHARLES MASON WAS RANKED FIRST IN their class, Lee was appointed adjutant, the highest leadership position a cadet could attain.

Joseph E. Johnston, who was Lee's classmate during their four years together at West Point, gave this description of his fellow cadet:

We had the same intimate associates who thought as I did that no other youth or man so united the qualities that win warm friendship and command high respect. For he was full of sympathy and kindness, genial and fond of gay conversation, and even of fun, while his correctness of demeanor and attention to all duties . . . gave him a superiority that everyone acknowledged in his heart. He was the only one of all the men I have known that could laugh at the faults and follies of his friends . . . without touching their affection for him.

A D V I C E

Consider more than technical proficiency when selecting someone for promotion to supervisor. Only raise from the ranks those who have earned the respect, and even affection, of their peers. Similarly, even the best academic record isn't sufficient justification, by itself, to recruit someone into a management trainee program.

8. BE IMPARTIAL

*L*EE BELIEVED THAT HIS SUCCESS AS A CADET OFFICER at West Point was due to the even-handed manner in which he had performed his duties. In an 1852 letter to his eldest son, who was then enrolled at West Point, Lee wrote that cadets in leadership positions must do their

> *duty, honestly and faithfully. Without favor and without partiality . . . The same as regards your dearest friend or worst enemy.*

In 1853, while Lee was Superintendent at West Point, his nephew, Fitzhugh, and several other cadets were caught off campus. Some of the boys were out of uniform and had liquor in their possession. Lee recommended that they all be dismissed from the Academy.

ADVICE

While Lee's advice applies to anyone in management, it pertains especially to those who are promoted from among their peers and given management responsibility for people who were previously their equals. By being scrupulously impartial, you will, in Lee's words, "gain esteem and affection and not dislike or hatred."

Fitzhugh was court-martialed and severely punished, but he was not dismissed and did graduate from West Point.

9. HAVE THEY EVER WORKED A DAY IN THEIR LIVES?

*W*ITHIN A MONTH OF HIS GRADUATION FROM WEST POINT, Lee's mother died. She had been the dominant influence in his life, and he often commented that he "owed everything" to her.

She believed that as children grow older they should be assigned increasing responsibilities. By the time Lee left for West Point, he was taking care of the family's affairs in a number of matters, from buying food and other supplies to caring for the animals and managing the family's expenses.

When Lee's older brother, Carter, spent more money in one year than had been budgeted for his entire college education, Lee's mother rebuked him in this sharply worded letter:

> *I am really astonished, confounded at your supposing that I could afford your entering into expenses at Cambridge, which I would not allow you at home . . . Was it not a doubtful question, whether I could, out of my annuity, give a college education to my sons, even if they pursued the most economical plan? . . . I had hoped you would be a highly educated discreet, judicious man. That you would have been an example for your brothers' imitation—a dignified protector for your sisters, and the pride and solace of your mother's declining years. But you are not pursuing the course to fulfill such expectations. He who prefers the gratification of sensual pleasures to the cultivation of mental endowments, will never be qualified for the performance of such duties.*

ADVICE

When filling management trainee positions with recent graduates, carefully consider the prior work experience of each applicant. Those who have helped to put themselves through school or had meaningful household responsibilities are more likely to understand the meaning of work and the value of money. They are your best candidates.

10. CAN THEY WRITE?

*L*EE'S MOTHER WROTE BEAUTIFUL LETTERS, AND SHE insisted that her sons be able to write well. When Lee's older brother, Smith, who was in the navy, failed to write, she took him to task:

> *My dear Smith, I have told you everything I thought interesting to you and now have arrived at the disagreeable point in my letter, the obligation I feel to chide you for never writing to your mother . . . but exclusive of my desire to hear from you, I lament your dislike of writing because it will be such a disadvantage to you through life. A man that cannot write a good letter . . . will find himself greatly at a loss on any occasion. . . . You must write often now in the days of your youth . . . if your letters are not well written at first you will improve after awhile.*

ADVICE

To be a successful manager, you need to be able to communicate clearly and concisely. If people who report to you haven't learned to write well, you would be doing your organization a disservice to promote them into management positions. A simple exercise for those who haven't been in jobs where they could demonstrate their writing skills is to ask them to prepare a one-page summary of a lengthy report. Clear, concise writing requires thought. In a letter to a friend, Mark Twain wrote, "If I'd had more time, it would have been shorter."

ENGINEERING HAD BEEN LEE'S FAVORITE SUBJECT AT West Point. His high class standing allowed him to choose the branch of service in which he would be commissioned a second lieutenant. Upon graduation he requested and received appointment to the Corps of Engineers. In the fall of 1829, Lee reported to his first post, Cockspur Island, where a fort was being built for the defense of Savannah, Georgia.

In addition to his engineering duties, Lee also served as post commissary. He found that being responsible for supplying provisions was an unglamorous and unrewarding assignment.

A D V I C E

There are some jobs that are only noticed when done badly, such as staff and support roles which are frequently taken for granted. Acknowledge all the people who contribute to your success. A little positive recognition from you will pay big dividends when you need something special from the often unappreciated folks in facilities, mail, security, fleet, food service, supply, maintenance or any of the other units upon which your area depends.

12. IS THE FOUNDATION SOLID?

*D*URING LEE'S SECOND YEAR AT COCKSPUR ISLAND, HIS commanding officer resigned due to poor health, and was replaced by First Lieutenant Joseph K. F. Mansfield. After careful study of the work that had been completed to that point, Mansfield concluded that the composition of the island's soil was unsuitable for the construction of the planned fortifications. Since all work would have to be suspended until Mansfield could draw up new plans, Lee was transferred to another post.

A D V I C E

Never blindly commit to someone else's plans. When you take over a project in mid-stream, begin at the beginning by making sure that the assumptions on which the project is based are still valid. If all you do is check progress to-date and work remaining, you may miss opportunities to flush out and correct deficiencies, redesign the project, or, in a worst case scenario, scrap it altogether.

Mansfield drew up new plans that were used in the construction of Fort Pulaski. He went on to command a Union army corps and was killed at the battle of Antietam (Sharpsburg).

13. LOOK, DON'T TOUCH

*I*N APRIL 1831, LEE WAS TRANSFERRED TO FORT MONROE, near Norfolk, Virginia. One of his favorite pastimes was going to the beach. He wrote to a friend:

> *As for the daughters of Eve in this country, they are formed in the very poetry of nature, and would make your lips water and fingers tingle. They are beginning to assemble to put their beautiful limbs into this salt water.*

Lee enjoyed being with women. He liked to look, and he liked to flirt. When asked about this, he responded:

> *You are right in my interest in pretty women, and it is strange I do not lose it with age.*

ADVICE

Don't expect people to leave their sex at the door when they come to work. It's perfectly natural to notice pretty women and handsome men. While you can't help looking, you can keep your thoughts to yourself. Managers must set the proper example. Those that engage in sexual innuendo are, at the very least, disrupting the workplace, and may even be creating an offensive or hostile work environment. They are a negative presence and have no place in management.

14. DON'T THROW OUT THE BABY WITH THE BATH WATER

*I*N AUGUST 1831, NAT TURNER, A SLAVE, ORGANIZED AND led a revolt. Troops from Fort Monroe were called out to suppress the rebellion, which was quickly crushed, but not before the slaves had killed more than sixty people. One aftermath of the revolt was that the commander of Fort Monroe issued an order forbidding all but a handful of blacks from entering the fort. Since the construction that Lee was supervising was carried out by contracted slave laborers, the order had the effect of bringing his work to a halt. Lee protested, and the order was withdrawn.

A D V I C E

You need to keep events in perspective, and be careful not to overreact. Otherwise, you may create a greater problem than the one you are reacting to.

Shortly after the revolt, a convention met to take up the issue of emancipation in Virginia. Fifty-eight of the delegates favored emancipation, sixty the continuation of slavery, and fourteen were undecided. The pro-slavery delegates were successful in using the revolt to raise fears that freed slaves would seek revenge on their former masters, and the undecided delegates voted with the pro-slavery faction.

15. THE STRAIN OF SEPARATION

$\mathcal{R}$OBERT E. LEE AND MARY CUSTIS WERE MARRIED ON June 30, 1831. Their first child was born in September 1832. Mary did not enjoy life at Fort Monroe, and she spent much of her time at her parents' home in Arlington, Virginia, a suburb of Washington, D.C. When Mary was away, Robert missed her, and he especially missed his young son.

My Sweet Little Boy—what I would give to see him! The house is a perfect desert without him. . . . I am waking all night to hear his sweet little voice, and if in the morning I could only feel his sweet little arms around my neck and his dear little heart fluttering against my breast, I should be too happy.

A D V I C E

Some jobs involve extensive travel requiring frequent and even extended family separation. Not everyone handles the strain of separation well. When making assignments be sensitive to a person's family circumstances. It's one thing to offer someone an opportunity; it's another to push a person to take a job that is going to cause great personal hardship. The result of doing that is likely to be lowered job performance.

Mary Custis was the daughter of George Washington's adopted son. She and Robert were distant relatives, and had been friends since childhood.

16. DRESSING FOR SUCCESS

*L*EE WAS VERY CONSCIOUS OF HIS APPEARANCE. HE WAS always well-dressed. While at Fort Monroe, he ordered a new dress uniform from a well-known tailor, and he asked his commanding officer, who was in New York at the time, to buy him a new hat.

My present Chapeau can be altered to the required shape in Norfolk. But I do not know whether I can obtain the necessary trimmings, consisting of a broad lace strap, Silver Eagle, Gilt lapels and ostrich feather . . . .

We shall be a grand set of fellows with our gold and silver . . . .

P.S. The circumference of my head is 22¹/₃ inches.

A D V I C E

It certainly never hurts to dress for success. But better dressed doesn't necessarily mean better qualified. As a manager, you must be careful not to mistake one for the other.

17. DISPIRITED TROOPS

*W*HILE LEE WAS BUSY CONSTRUCTING THE FORTIFICATIONS at Fort Monroe, he observed that many of his fellow officers were not gainfully employed and had too much idle time on their hands.

My opinion on these matters has been formed, from the little experience I have had of a Garrison life in time of peace, where I have seen minds . . . degenerate into sluggishness and inactivity, requiring the stimulus of brandy or cards to rouse them to action.

A D V I C E

Managers who fail to provide meaningful and challenging work end up with disgruntled and dispirited people. During slow periods do the things that you never have enough time for, such as updating documentation, doing practice exercises and providing extra training.

18. TURF SQUABBLES

*T*HE CORPS OF ENGINEERS HAD CONSIDERABLE
autonomy in contracting for labor and materials. Since
other army units had no such latitude, this became a source
of resentment and friction. During Lee's time at Fort
Monroe, there were several disputes and almost constant
sniping between the engineers and the rest of the garrison.
This so discouraged Lee that he requested a transfer.

*As much as I like the location . . . and as fond as I am
of the company of some of the officers and of some persons
in the neighborhood and notwithstanding the great partiali-
ty I have for my commanding officer (I mean no flattery)
and my belief I shall not meet with such another —yet there
are so many . . . disagreements connected with the duty that
I should like to get another post.*

Lee wrote to a friend that he was even considering
resigning from the army.

*Know, my friend, that it is a situation full of pains, and
one from which I shall modestly retire on the first fitting
opportunity.*

A D V I C E

Inter-unit disputes demoralize people. Constant turf squab-
bles will cost you your best people. As a manager, It's your
responsibility to set a cooperative tone. Avoid making
remarks and taking actions that foster petty jealousies and
unprofessional attitudes and conduct. If you see a quarrel
developing between your people and those from another
unit, don't let it fester. Nip it in the bud.

19. DON'T TAKE IT PERSONALLY

IN JULY 1834, THE COMMANDING GENERAL OF THE ARMY, Alexander Macomb, inspected the fortifications at Fort Monroe. He concluded that the services of the engineers were no longer required and that the remaining work could be completed under the direction of the commandant of the fort.

Lee and his superiors were upset with this decision. They felt General Macomb's order was unjustly critical of their efforts. The head of the Corps of Engineers requested a formal inquiry, but General Macomb denied his request on the grounds that no investigation was necessary.

For my part, I cannot see that any censure is either expressed or implied . . . and I am sure none was intended.

ADVICE

When a decision doesn't go your way, don't jump to the conclusion that it's a reflection on your performance. Reasonable people can disagree on the best course for the future without implying or intending any criticism of past actions. If you take every adverse decision personally, you will become embittered and frustrated and your work will suffer.

20. GET A BACKSTOP

*I*N THE AUTUMN OF 1834, LEE WAS OFFERED THE opportunity to become an assistant to General Charles Gratiot, the head of the Corps of Engineers. He reluctantly accepted the assignment. He wanted to get away from Fort Monroe, but he knew that paper-pushing was not his cup of tea.

I abhor the sight of pen and paper and to put one t'other requires as great a moral effort as for a cat to walk on hot coals.

When Lee left for Washington, D.C. to take up his new duties, he took with him the clerk who had handled the accounting and correspondence for him at Fort Monroe.

A D V I C E

If there are things you don't do well, get someone to help you do them. Also, don't hesitate to backstop any of your people who may need assistance with certain kinds of tasks.

21. YOU ARE NOT INDISPENSABLE

*I*N THE SPRING OF 1835, LEE TOOK PART IN A SURVEY OF the Ohio-Michigan state line. Because of bad weather, the survey progressed more slowly than planned, and Lee did not reach Detroit until mid-August. There he received a letter from his wife, who had become ill after the birth of their daughter, Mary, in July. She wanted him to return home immediately. Lee responded:

But why do you urge my immediate return, and tempt one in the strongest manner, to endeavor to get excused from the performance of a duty, imposed on me by my profession, for the pure gratification of my private feelings? . . . I am [not] one of those fair weather gentlemen whose duty and pleasure must go together; or that if I should be called on to sacrifice the latter, I cannot be trusted to execute the former. . . . You see therefore dear Mary, that however strongly I may be tempted by my own feelings, backed by your request, I cannot in conscience do what you ask. And that however harassing will be to me the idea that your recovery may be retarded by a delay of my return, I must not consent to do aught that would lower me in your eyes, my own and that of others.

Lee returned home in October to find his wife gravely ill.

A D V I C E

Charles de Gaulle said, "Graveyards are filled with indispensable people." Your work is important, but your family should come first. Whatever you are doing can temporarily be turned over to someone else.

Mary's letter was written in Arlington, Virginia on August 13th; Lee's reply from Detroit, Michigan was dated August 21st, which speaks well for the efficiency of the U.S. Postal Department in 1835.

22. LOBBYING CONGRESS

*L*EE WAS NOT PROMOTED TO FIRST LIEUTENANT UNTIL
September 1836, seven years after graduating from West
Point. He felt the Corps of Engineers was being "horribly,
shamefully treated" by Congress.

*You ask what are my prospects in the Corps? Bad
enough–unless . . . something [is] done for us, and then perhaps they will be better.*

Lee tried his hand at lobbying Congress on behalf of
the Corps of Engineers, but without success.

A D V I C E

Some members of Congress have a 20-second sound-bite
attention span. Others, when dealing with people who have
neither large sums of money to contribute nor blocs of
votes to deliver, pay even less attention. Inexperienced juniors, no matter how ardent or sincere, have no business
swimming with Washington sharks. Send only seasoned lob-
byists to do battle in the Capitol.

Lee did not enjoy working in Washington: "I was cognizant of so much iniqui-
ty in more ways than one, that I feared for my morality."

2

THE WORK
WASN'T WASTED

August 1837 – August 1846

As a supervising engineer, Lee begins construction of
a system of dikes designed to save the St. Louis harbor.
While he is frustrated by the failure of Congress to
appropriate funds for the completion of the project,
the city is grateful for his efforts to control the
Mississippi River.

23. PROMISES, PROMISES

*I*N EARLY AUGUST 1837, LEE AND HIS ASSISTANT, SECOND Lieutenant Montgomery C. Meigs, arrived in St. Louis, Missouri to begin a new assignment. En-route, Lee stopped in Louisville, Kentucky to inspect several boats that were being constructed for his use. He was told that the boats were nearly ready and would be sent to St. Louis in a few days. Lee could not begin his surveys of the river without these boats, and he showed his frustration when they did not arrive on time.

They are the greatest people for promising and not fulfilling, that I ever saw. Never hesitate to undertake anything, but completing is another matter.

ADVICE

Supplier delays are costly. While penalty and exit provisions in supplier contracts can help to mitigate your damages, they are a poor remedy for nonperformance. Where performance is critical, deal only with those who have a proven track record of delivering on time and as promised.

During the Civil War, Meigs, who was from Georgia, served as Quartermaster General for the Union. He was responsible for converting the grounds of Lee's estate in Arlington into a national cemetery.

$\mathscr{S}$INCE LEE'S WIFE HAD GIVEN BIRTH IN MAY, SHE DID not accompany him to St. Louis. She remained in Arlington with their five-year-old son, one-year-old daughter and the newborn infant. Lee wrote concerning their son:

> *Our dear little boy seems to have . . . a reputation of being hard to manage—a distinction not at all desirable, as it indicates self-will and obstinacy . . . but it is our duty, if possible, to counteract them and assist him to bring them under his control. I have endeavored . . . to require nothing but what was in my opinion necessary or proper, and to explain to him temperately its propriety, at a time when he could listen to my arguments, and not at the moment of his being vexed and his little faculties warped by passion. I have also tried to show him that I was firm in my demands, and constant in their enforcement, and that he must comply with them.*

ADVICE

Lee's advice for dealing with the behavior of a headstrong five-year-old applies equally well to dealing with immature behavior at any age.

25. EASIER SAID THAN DONE

*I*F LEE HAD GIVEN THE IMPRESSION THAT HE HAD mastered the art of managing the behavior of a five-year-old, he was quick to set the record straight:

> *Since my efforts have been so unsuccessful, I fear I have altogether failed in accomplishing my purpose, but I hope to be able to profit from my experience. . . . I am ready to acknowledge the good advice contained in the text-books, and I believe that I see the merit of their reasoning generally; but what I want to learn is to apply what I already know.*

ADVICE

Managing others can be both incredibly frustrating and rewarding. Even when they are not your children, it is never easy. To develop their leadership skills, provide your people with practical management training that they can apply to their work. Role-playing sessions that expose new supervisors to confrontational situations are especially valuable.

26. TAKE A SECOND LOOK

HE COURSE OF THE MISSISSIPPI RIVER HAD GRADUALLY shifted, creating two large islands that were diverting the current to the Illinois bank of the river. Unless checked, the water on the Missouri side of the river would become too shallow for navigation. Mississippi riverboats would no longer be able to dock in St. Louis, and the young city might become a ghost town. To prevent that from happening, Lee decided to build dikes that would divert the current to the Missouri side of the river.

Lee's original plan, drawn up in the fall of 1837, called for the construction of one dike that would extend at a right angle from the Illinois shoreline. Before beginning construction a year later, Lee took another look at his plan. He concluded that he had underestimated the strength of the current, and the dike he had planned to build might be washed away. Instead Lee now proposed to build a dike that would be anchored by the Illinois bank on one end and by an island on the other.

ADVICE

Even if you developed the project plan, still take a second look. It is especially important to do so whenever a considerable period of time has elapsed between the formulation of a plan and the start of its implementation.

27. FAMILIARITY BREEDS CONTEMPT

*T*HE MAYOR OF ST. LOUIS, JOHN F. DARBY, OBSERVED the construction of the dikes. He wrote that Lee

> *went in person with the hands every morning about sunrise, and worked day by day in the hot, broiling sun. . . . He shared in the hard task and common fare and rations furnished to the common laborers —eating at the same table in the cabin of the steamboat used in the prosecution of the work, but never on any occasion becoming too familiar with the men. He maintained and preserved under all circumstances his dignity and gentlemanly bearing, winning and commanding the esteem, regard, and respect of every one under him.*

A D V I C E

There is a lot of truth in the old saying that familiarity breeds contempt. Even in close quarters, learn to keep your distance by being selective about what you say and what you choose to hear.

28. POLITICAL FOOTBALLS

*T*HE SUBJECT OF APPROPRIATIONS FOR LEE'S PROJECT became a hot issue in the local political elections of 1838. When asked to comment, Lee said:

The government has sent me here as an officer of the army to do a certain work. I shall do it.

The manner in which Lee conducted himself throughout the election campaign earned him widespread approval. One newspaper reporter wrote that Lee

deported himself throughout our election as every government officer should, but as very few at this day do, taking no part in the contest.

ADVICE

If your project becomes a political football, try to avoid being drawn into the public debate. If you have to become involved, hire professional help to make your case. You have neither the expertise nor the time to get involved in public wrangling with politicians and the media.

29. PROCRASTINATION

*I*N AUGUST 1838, LEE WAS PROMOTED TO CAPTAIN. HE viewed his promotion as a mixed blessing.

> *I do not know whether I ought to rejoice or not . . . as in all my schemes of happiness I look forward to returning to some quiet corner among the hills of Virginia where I can indulge my natural propensities without interruption, and I suppose the more comfortably I am fixed in the army, the less likely I shall be to leave it.*

After the Civil War, Lee would conclude that the greatest mistake of his life was remaining in the army.

ADVICE

If you're considering a career change, don't procrastinate. You can always find an excuse not to leave a secure and comfortable position and strike out in a new direction. Comfortable and happy are not necessarily synonymous. While you may be able to go back to your old job if you decide the change was a mistake, you won't be able to undo the remorse you'll feel later in life for never having tried the new field.

30. WHAT ARE THEY REALLY AFTER?

*I*N DECEMBER 1838, LEE'S BOSS, GENERAL CHARLES Gratiot, was accused of fraud and dismissed from the army. Lee held Gratiot in high regard and was shocked by the news. He wrote to a friend:

> *I believe the news of his death would have been less painful to me. Nor when I call to mind his zeal and integrity in the discharge of his duties . . . can I either comprehend or account for a result that has deprived the country of so valuable an officer.*

General Gratiot was not tried until 1841, and while he was cleared of all charges, he was never restored to active duty. He ended up working as a clerk in the General Land Office in Washington.

Lee believed that the accusation of fraud had been a pretext to remove Gratiot from his position as chief of the Corps of Engineers. He felt that Gratiot had

> *failed in the beginning of his controversy to penetrate the designs of his enemies and study to refute them.*

ADVICE

If you find yourself under attack, make it your number one priority to figure out what the other side really wants. Without that knowledge, you are at a great disadvantage, and it will be extremely difficult, if not impossible, to achieve a favorable outcome.

31. THERE'S MORE THAN ONE WAY TO SKIN A CAT

*D*URING THE SUMMER OF 1839, A LAND SPECULATOR with plans to develop property on the Illinois side of the river obtained an injunction that required the Corps of Engineers to suspend work on the dike being built from the Illinois shore. Lee did not believe the complainant's assertion that property values on the Illinois side of the river would fall if the dike was completed. However, his request to have the injunction vacated could not be heard by the court until after the onset of winter, when construction would have to be halted due to the weather. Since only the United States government was enjoined from continuing construction, Lee turned the work over to the city of St. Louis. Construction continued under the supervision of Lee's civilian assistant who used equipment

loaned by Captain R. E. Lee, Corps of Engineers, as Agent of the United States to the City of St. Louis.

ADVICE

If you keep your focus on getting the job done, you will usually be able to find the means to get around any roadblocks that are placed in your path.

IN THE SUMMER OF 1839, LEE WAS OFFERED AN opportunity to teach at West Point. He refused the position, much to the dismay of his superior who had recommended him for the post.

It would have been uncandid to have induced him to believe that I possessed the taste and peculiar zeal which the situation requires, nor can I see what qualifications I possess that renders me more fit for this duty than others.

ADVICE

If you are permitted to refuse an assignment that's not to your liking, then do so, especially if you would bring no special qualifications to the task.

33. THE WORK WASN'T WASTED

*I*N 1840, CONGRESS ADJOURNED WITHOUT APPROPRIATING funds to complete the Mississippi River improvements that Lee was supervising. The project was cancelled, and Lee was reassigned. As the mayor of St. Louis, John F. Darby, recalled, Lee was not happy with the decision:

> *Lee expressed to me his chagrin and mortification at being compelled to discontinue the work. It seemed as if it were a great personal misfortune to stop, when the work was about half finished.*

While Lee did not get to complete the work he had started, he had accomplished a great deal, and Mayor Darby made sure Lee understood

> *the great obligation the authorities and citizens generally were under to him, for his skill and labor in preserving the harbor.*

A D V I C E

Sometimes an incomplete project can produce meaningful results. Even when it doesn't, the work is still not totally wasted if you have learned and grown from the experience.

Control of the Mississippi River at St. Louis is still based on the work that Lee began in 1837.

34. SENSITIVE SUBJECTS

*I*N APRIL 1841, LEE ARRIVED AT FORT HAMILTON, New York. His assignment was to oversee repairs and improvements to the forts that defended the entrance to New York City's harbor. While at Fort Hamilton, Lee was a vestryman at the fort's Episcopal Church. The congregation was hotly divided over Puseyism, the teachings of the Oxford theologian, Edward B. Pusey. Lee refused to state his position on the matter. As one of his friends, Second Lieutenant Henry J. Hunt, recalled, whenever the officers at the fort gathered to discuss the subject

[Lee] always contrived in some pleasant way to avoid any expression of opinion that would commit him to either faction. One evening . . . the inevitable subject came up and was discussed with considerable warmth. . . . Captain Lee was quiet, but to those who understood him, evidently amused at the efforts to draw him out.

Lee decided to use humor to defuse the situation. He turned to Hunt and said in a mock serious tone of voice:

I am glad to see that you keep aloof from the dispute that is disturbing our little parish. That is right, and we must not get mixed up in it; we must support each other in that. But I must give you some advice about it, in order that we may understand each other: Beware of Pussyism!

ADVICE

At work, don't discuss sensitive subjects, such as politics or religion. Often, humor can be used to deflect the heated feelings generated by such discussions, and to help you move on to less volatile subjects.

Hunt played a prominent role in revising field artillery tactics. As major general and chief of artillery for the Union Army of the Potomac, he is credited with breaking the back of Lee's assaults at Malvern Hill and on the final day at Gettysburg.

35. SPECIAL ASSIGNMENTS

*I*N 1844, LEE WAS APPOINTED TO THE BOARD OF ARMY officers that would oversee that year's annual examinations at West Point. The following year he became a member of the board of engineers that was reviewing the nation's Atlantic coast defenses. These assignments, which were in addition to his regular duties, brought Lee into close contact with some of the leading men of the army.

It was during this period that Lee became closely acquainted with Major General Winfield Scott, who had become the army's commanding general in 1841. He was known as "Old Fuss and Feathers" because of his love of showy uniforms, but he was a fine judge of men. Scott was the president of the board of examiners to which Lee had been appointed. He had the opportunity to observe Lee closely, and he was favorably impressed by what he saw. Over time, Scott's opinion would have a profound influence upon Lee's future.

ADVICE

Look to take on special assignments, particularly if they bring you into contact with the senior members of the organization. Not only do they provide an opportunity for you to demonstrate your abilities and character, they also offer unparalleled opportunities for learning. Committee and task force assignments offer invaluable training because they help you to develop essential leadership skills for dealing with people at all levels.

36. DON'T MAKE A FEDERAL CASE OUT OF IT

*L*EE DID NOT ENJOY BOOKKEEPING. AS A RESULT OF AN error on his part, Lee received double the pay he was entitled to for two months in 1845. After the error was discovered, the money was quickly repaid. While it was dismissed by Lee's superior as nothing more than a simple accounting error, Lee was greatly troubled by his failure.

It has caused me more mortification than any other act of my life, to find that I have been culpably negligent where the strictest accuracy is both necessary and required.

ADVICE

Treat mistakes, both yours and those made by others, as learning opportunities. You don't need to make a federal case out of an easily correctable mistake. The person who committed the error will feel bad enough without your adding to his or her misery and embarrassment.

37. ROLE MODEL

$\mathcal{R}$OBERT AND MARY LEE HAD SEVEN CHILDREN, THREE boys and four girls. When their eldest boy was still quite young, Lee took him for a walk in the snow. After a while, the boy started to lag behind. Looking back over his shoulder, Lee observed his son walking in his father's footprints and trying to mimic his every action. As Lee later recalled:

When I saw this, I said to myself, "It behooves me to walk very straight when this fellow is already following in my tracks."

ADVICE

Just as parents are role models for their children, managers are role models for the people that report to them. Your every action is observed and scrutinized. You need to behave as if you were constantly on camera or on stage, for, in truth, you are.

SUPER HERO

August 1846–June 1848

During the Mexican War, Lee performs brilliantly.
Winfield Scott, the army's commander, calls him "the
very best soldier I ever saw in the field" and says that
American "success in Mexico was largely due to the skill,
valor and undaunted energy of Robert E. Lee."

38. KEEP THEIR SKILLS HONED

*O*N MAY 13, 1846, THE UNITED STATES DECLARED WAR on Mexico. In August, Lee was ordered to report to Brigadier General John E. Wool in San Antonio, Texas. Wool was under the command of Major General Zachary Taylor, who had already invaded Mexico and was marching on Monterrey.

When Wool's command began its march to Mexico, Lee was with troops in the field for the first time since he had graduated from West Point seventeen years earlier.

ADVICE

People's skills deteriorate when not used regularly. While there are exceptional people who can pick up where their training and experience left off without missing a beat, don't assume that this is true for your people. Keep their skills sharpened through training exercises. This is particularly important in a changing field where what was learned even a short time ago can quickly become obsolete.

39. RATIONALIZATIONS

*B*EFORE LEAVING FOR MEXICO, LEE WROTE HIS WILL. Upon his death, his slaves were to be

liberated so soon as it can be done to their advantage.

In a letter, written in 1856, Lee expressed the view that

slavery as an institution is a moral and political evil. . . . The blacks are immeasurably better off here than in Africa, morally, socially and physically. The painful discipline they are undergoing is necessary for their instruction as a race, and I hope will prepare and lead them to better things. How long their subjugation may be necessary is known and ordered by a wise Merciful Providence. . . . While we see the course of the final abolition of human slavery is onward, and we give it the aid of our prayers and all justifiable means in our power, we must leave the progress as well as the result in His hands who sees the end, who chooses to work by slow influences, and with whom two thousand years are but a single day.

ADVICE

When considering a proposal, some executives only ask if it's feasible, practical and legal. They develop rationalizations to justify unethical practices, because they view them as essential short-term measures on the road to accomplishing important goals. But "legal" and "ethical" are not synonyms.

40. DON'T STOP AT MIDFIELD

*A*FTER CAPTURING MONTERREY (SEPTEMBER 24, 1846), General Taylor had agreed to an armistice. As a result General Wool's advance was halted for nearly a month. Lee thought that Taylor had made a mistake in agreeing to an armistice.

I am one of those silly persons that when I have any-thing to do I can't rest satisfied until it has been accom-plished. And it has appeared to me that we have been losing time important to us and granting a season of preparation to the Mexicans. If then they were so crippled by the battle of Monterrey, by all means advantage should have been taken of our success, and perhaps the whole Mexican army would have fallen into our hands. Whereas I now fear time has been given them to recover at least partially from that blow and that when hostilities are resumed, they will be found stronger and we weaker from the respite.

ADVICE

If you let up, you will lose momentum, while your competi-tors will have the opportunity to catch their breath and regroup.

41. LITTLE THINGS MEAN A LOT

*W*HEN LEE WENT OFF TO WAR, HIS FATHER-IN-LAW GAVE him the family's "Revolutionary knives and forks," the ones that George Washington had used in the field. When General Wool's staff sat down to Christmas dinner, they found that Lee had lent a piece of Washington's cutlery for each place setting. The pieces

were passed around the table with much veneration and excited universal admiration.

A D V I C E

A simple, seemingly minor, gesture can make a difference in a person's attitude and performance. Monetary rewards are important, but psychological rewards can be even more significant. You are unlikely to have historic or art treasures to share with your staff, but there are numerous other things that will mean a great deal. Managers who show kindness in little ways earn huge rewards in staff loyalty and performance.

42. CHECK OUT THE FACTS

*I*N ADDITION TO HIS ENGINEERING DUTIES, WHICH consisted of constructing roads, bridges and earthworks, Lee served as a scout. One night, there were reports that a large Mexican force was approaching. Lee, with a guide, went out to ascertain the enemy's position.

Years later, Lee related the story of his reconnaissance to the Reverend J. William Jones. As Jones recalled, Lee found tracks of mules and wagons within five miles of the point at which the Mexicans had been sighted. A little further on, he saw a large number of campfires on a hillside. Lee's guide was convinced that they were within the lines of the whole Mexican army and, fearing capture, he pleaded with him to return to General Wool's camp. Lee wanted to be certain that he had found the Mexicans. He moved toward their white tents, getting within earshot.

Here he discovered that his "white tents" were an immense flock of sheep, and that the supposed army was simply a large train of wagons, and a herd of cattle, mules, etc., being driven to market.

A D V I C E

Don't jump to premature conclusions. Take the time and effort to thoroughly check the facts. Otherwise, you could end up looking like a fool or sending your organization on a wild goose chase.

43. WILD ACCOUNTS

HERE SEEMED TO BE NO END OF REPORTS THAT AN attack by the Mexican army was imminent. One day when Lee was at General Taylor's headquarters, an officer rushed in to report that he had seen the Mexican army, 20,000 men and 250 cannon. As Lee recalled, Taylor asked:

Captain, do you say that you saw that force?

Yes, General.

Captain, if you say you saw it, of course I must believe you; but I would not have believed it if I had seen it myself.

ADVICE

Wild rumors can at times run like brush fires through an organization. Keep your focus. You can't afford to be distracted by panicked imaginings. Also, help your people stay focused by making sure they know the facts.

44. END GAME

PRESIDENT JAMES K. POLK HAD TAKEN THE UNITED States to war with Mexico. His aim was to seize the territories of California and New Mexico and gain control of northern Mexico, at least as far south as the Rio Grande River. When this was accomplished, he thought the war would be over, but it wasn't. The Mexicans, in spite of the defeats they had suffered on the battlefield, did not sue for peace, and the United States had no alternate plan for ending the war. Finally, in November 1846, Winfield Scott, the army's commanding general, drew up a plan for landing at Vera Cruz, marching inland and capturing Mexico City. This, he convinced the President, would bring the war to a close.

ADVICE

You need an end game. You can't win in business or anything else with only an opening gambit. Remember Sir Francis Drake's prayer, "Oh Lord, when thou entrust thy servants to endeavor some great matter, give us also to understand that it is not the beginning but the continuing through of the same until it be thoroughly concluded which yields the true glory."

45. DON'T GIVE THEM A BEACH-HEAD

*I*N JANUARY 1847, LEE RECEIVED ORDERS TO JOIN THE Vera Cruz invasion force as a member of Scott's personal staff. Scott was anxious to capture Vera Cruz and move inland as quickly as possible. He feared that if he were detained into April by Mexican resistance at Vera Cruz, an outbreak of yellow fever, which marked the onset of hot weather, would come to the aid of the enemy and destroy his army. After some delay, the invasion fleet was assembled and made its way down the coast, arriving off Vera Cruz on March 5th.

Late in the afternoon on March 9th, American infantry climbed into their landing boats and began to make their way toward a beach southeast of the city. Everyone expected that the Mexicans would try to prevent the landing. Every eye was trained on the landing craft, causing one soldier to write that it reminded him of

crows on trees, watching the dead carcass beneath.

To everyone's surprise, the landing was unopposed. The Mexican defenders remained behind their city walls and, without firing a shot, allowed Scott's army to establish a beachhead and land the troops, artillery and supplies needed to besiege the city.

A D V I C E

If your competitors challenge you, you can't afford to lay back. Once you let them get a toehold in your marketplace, it's nearly impossible to drive them out. If you hope to successfully beat back the competition, you need to meet their challenge the moment you become aware of it. That is when they are at their weakest and you have the best opportunity to throw them off base, disrupt their timing and frustrate their plans.

46. RECOGNIZE WHEN YOU ARE OUT OF YOUR ELEMENT

*D*URING THE SIEGE OF VERA CRUZ, LEE WAS RESPONSIBLE for the placement of a battery of heavy naval guns that had been borrowed from the fleet. To protect the guns, Lee ordered the seamen who manned them to construct embankments. The sailors were not happy at the prospect, and their commanding officer protested.

The boys don't want any dirt to hide behind. They only want to get at the enemy, and after you have finished your banks we will not stay behind them—we will get up on top where we can have a fair fight.

During the bombardment, the Mexicans concentrated their fire on Lee's naval battery. When the shelling stopped, the naval officer who had objected to constructing earthworks because his men had not "enlisted to dig dirt" said to Lee:

I suppose the dirt did save some of my boys from being killed or wounded. But I knew that we would have no use for dirt banks on shipboard—there what we want is clear decks and an open sea. And the fact is, Captain, I don't like this land fighting anyway. It ain't clean!

ADVICE

If you find yourself in unfamiliar waters, listen to those who know the territory. Respect the differences inherent in operating in different businesses, locales or environments, and don't blindly try to apply what works in one to another. This is particularly important if you are brought in to manage an organization in a field in which you have no prior experience. You need to learn the rudiments of the new business in order to understand what should and should not be applied from your previous experience.

47. ON SEEING OTHERS PROMOTED

*S*HORTLY AFTER VERA CRUZ SURRENDERED
(March 29, 1847), Lee's old buddy, Joseph E. Johnston,
received a brevet (temporary) promotion to lieutenant
colonel. Lee wrote his wife:

It is a fine thing to have strong friends in our govern-
ment, and I am glad that some of our friends have felt the
benefit of it.

A D V I C E

It's not always easy to be pleased when your friends and
peers are promoted, especially if the promotion was one
you were hoping for yourself. If you can't be pleased, you
can at least appear pleased. Showing bitterness will cost you
a friend and lessen your chances for a future promotion.

$\mathscr{S}$COTT'S ARMY BEGAN ITS MARCH INLAND. TO STOP THE American advance, the Mexicans established a defensive line in the mountain passes. As Lee described it:

> *The right of the Mexican line rested on the river at a perpendicular rock, unscalable by man or beast, and their left on impassable ravines . . . in their rear was the mountain of Cerro Gordo, surrounded by entrenchments in which were cannon, and crowned by a tower overlooking all. . . . I reconnoitered the ground in the direction of the ravines on their left.*

While searching for a path that would enable the Americans to outflank the Mexican defenders, Lee barely avoided being captured or killed. He was standing by a spring when he heard a group of Mexican soldiers approaching. Hiding beneath a fallen log, he waited for them to fill their canteens and leave. It proved to be a long wait. During the course of the day, the area around the spring was crowded with Mexican soldiers. Some sat on the log under which Lee was hiding; others stepped over it and nearly stepped on Lee. It was nightfall before he was able to slip away and return to Scott's headquarters.

ADVICE

We all get lucky breaks and are thankful for them, but we can never be certain when Lady Luck will smile on us. One of the most serious mistakes a manager can make is to develop plans that he or she knows will require a little luck to succeed. You'll need luck for all the things you haven't thought about, the unanticipated events. If you need luck to do the things you have planned, you are probably starting out so far behind the eight ball that you don't have a realistic chance of being successful.

Lee's reconnaissance paved the way for the American victory in the battle of Cerro Gordo (April 17–18, 1847). In his report of the battle, Scott singled Lee out for praise, and he received a brevet promotion to major.

49. SUPER HERO

*A*FTER THEIR DEFEAT AT CERRO GORDO, THE Mexicans established their defenses at Contreras and Churubusco. Between the roads leading to these two towns was a huge lava field called the Pedregal. One American soldier wrote that it looked like "a sea, which having been lashed into fury by a tempest, had been suddenly transformed . . . into stone." It was considered impassable, but Lee found a path, and on the morning of August 19th led part of the American army behind the Mexican defenders at Contreras. That night, during a thunderstorm, he recrossed the Pedregal and reported to Scott, who noted in his report:

Of the seven officers dispatched since sundown, from my position . . . on this side of the volcanic field...not one has succeeded in getting through. . . . They have all returned. But the gallant and indefatigable Captain Lee of the Engineers . . . [having crossed the lava field from the other side] is (eleven o'clock p.m.) just in.

Lee then crossed the Pedregal for a second time that night leading additional troops into position for an attack on Contreras the next morning. He then re-crossed the lava field again and directed troops into a position from which to attack the Mexican flank at Churubusco. After the American victory Lee, who had been without sleep for thirty-six hours, joined in the pursuit of the fleeing Mexicans. For his actions, he received a brevet promotion to lieutenant colonel. Scott called Lee's performance "the greatest feat of physical and moral courage performed by any individual" during the war.

A D V I C E

Sometimes you have to ask your staff to act like super heroes, working extra long hours and going without rest, to get a critically important job done. Don't make a habit of it. It should be the exception and not the norm, because super hero performance is not sustainable over extended periods of time.

50. HISTORY IS THE BEST TEACHER

*A*FTER THE AMERICAN VICTORIES AT CONTRERAS AND Churubusco, the Mexicans requested an armistice. Scott agreed, and hostilities ceased on August 24, 1847. The stated purpose of the armistice was to give American and Mexican negotiators the opportunity to conclude a peace treaty. Under the terms of the armistice, neither side was to engage in any military activities such as constructing or reinforcing defensive positions. By September 7th, it was clear that Scott had been deceived. The Mexicans, instead of negotiating in good faith, had been using the opportunity afforded by the armistice to regroup and strengthen the defenses guarding the approaches to Mexico City.

General Taylor had made the mistake earlier in the war of granting an armistice that the Mexicans had used to their advantage, but Scott had failed to learn from Taylor's experience. When hostilities were resumed, the Americans went on to win the battles of Molino del Rey (September 8th) and Chapultepec (September 13th). However, these victories were achieved at a far greater cost than would have been the case had the Americans not given the Mexicans the opportunity to recover from their earlier defeats by agreeing to an armistice. Scott was perhaps thinking of this when, after Mexico City surrendered (September 14th), he said to his staff:

Gentlemen, we must not be too elated by our success.

ADVICE

It is a lot less painful to learn from someone else's mistakes than from your own. Harry Truman said, "The only thing new in the world is the history you don't know." History can be your best teacher, but only if you understand its lessons.

For his services at the battle of Chapultepec, Lee received a brevet promotion to colonel.

51. LISTEN, THEN DECIDE

*I*N DEVELOPING HIS PLANS TO CAPTURE MEXICO CITY, Scott had to choose between attacking the western or the southern gates to the city. An attack from the west would require assaulting the fortress of Chapultepec. Scott favored the western approach, and he presented his proposed plan at a meeting of his staff. He asked his subordinates to freely express their views. Lee and most of the officers present favored the southern approach. When everyone had been heard, Scott concluded the meeting by asking his staff "to remain here for further orders." He then retired to make his decision. When he returned, he announced the attack would be made from the west.

ADVICE

Margaret Thatcher said, "Consensus is the absence of leadership." If the decision can be made by taking a vote or by making compromises until unanimous consent is achieved, you probably aren't deciding something that is important. For minor matters, like where to hold the Christmas party, it's perfectly okay to decide by taking a vote. But you have to make the important decisions yourself. You should listen to your staff. Their input may have a critical bearing on your thinking, but you have the ultimate responsibility for the outcome.

52. CLAIM JUMPERS

ON THE MORNING OF SEPTEMBER 13TH, LEE WAS GUIDING General Gideon J. Pillow and his troops to the position from which they were to make the assault on the fortress of Chapultepec. Suddenly Pillow announced that he had been wounded and needed to go to a field hospital. Lee believed that the only way in which Pillow could have been wounded at that moment was if an enemy musket ball had bounced off a tree before hitting him. Pillow reportedly claimed that his leg had been shattered, but the army doctors who examined him found that he was uninjured.

It is so much more easy to make heroes on paper than in the field. For one of the latter you meet with 20 of the former, but not till the fight is done. The fine fellows are too precious . . . to expose them to the view of the enemy, but when the battle is won, they accomplish with the tongue all that they would have done with the sword, had it not been dangerous to do so.

ADVICE

Some people talk a great game. They perform very effectively in interviews and social settings, but not on the job. Be leery of managerial candidates who use all the latest buzzwords (e.g., best practices, competing through competence, knowledge imperative, reengineering, thought leadership, transformation management) but whose prior performance cannot be verified or has to be explained away.

During the Civil War, Ulysses S. Grant relied on Pillow's reputation for cowardice in making his plans to capture Fort Donelson. When the fort surrendered (February 16, 1862), he learned that Pillow had escaped. Grant told a Confederate officer that if he had captured Pillow he "would have turned him loose. I would rather have him in command of you fellows than a prisoner."

53. SOUR SUCCESS

$\mathcal{N}$O SOONER HAD THE AMERICAN ARMY WON THE WAR than its commanding officers began a new war—with each other. General Pillow filed a report that Scott felt was in error. There were several heated exchanges, followed by charges and countercharges. Other officers were drawn into the quarrel, which reverberated from Mexico City to Washington, D.C. Scott placed Pillow under arrest for insubordination, and he was ordered to stand trial by court-martial. President Polk relieved Scott of command and ordered him to appear before a court of inquiry. Lee believed that the dispute had cast a dark shadow over what was otherwise a brilliant victory.

It is a contest in which neither party has anything to gain and the army much to lose, and ought to have been avoided.

Pillow was acquitted, and Scott was exonerated, but the dispute left a sour taste that lingered for some time.

ADVICE

When someone makes inaccurate statements, you need to set the record straight, but don't get into a pissing contest, because then everyone loses.

*L*EE THOUGHT THAT RELIEVING SCOTT OF COMMAND ON the basis of unsubstantiated charges had been a serious mistake. Scott had won the war in Mexico, and Lee felt he deserved

> *every support and confidence from his government at home. If he abused his trust or authority, it is then time to hold him to account. But . . . to suspend a successful general in command of an army in the heart of an enemy's country . . . is to upset all discipline; to jeopardize the safety of the army and the honor of the country, and to violate justice.*

Scott, who was ambitious, had made no secret of the fact that he had his eye on a run for the presidency. President Polk was looking for any excuse to damage a potential political opponent. When Scott overreacted to Pillow's statements, thereby blowing a minor matter all out of proportion, he gave Polk the opportunity he was waiting for.

A D V I C E

Some chief executive officers are so insecure that it's the kiss of death to be mentioned as their possible successor. Competence and loyalty don't count when they feel threatened. No sooner is someone mentioned in the press as a potential heir apparent than the people in the organization begin taking bets on when that person will be gone. You want ambitious people working for you, and it is natural for them to aspire to your job. Just as you should not tolerate back-stabbing, you should not practice it.

55. TEACH, TEACH, TEACH

*L*EE BELIEVED THAT AMERICAN SUCCESS IN MEXICO was due to General Scott's leadership.

It was his stout heart . . . his bold self-reliance . . . his indomitable courage that amid all the doubts and difficulties that surrounded us . . . pressed forward to this Capital [Mexico City], and finally brought us within its gates.

One could learn a great deal just from observing the way in which Scott led the army, and Lee did. Scott understood the importance of preparing his subordinates for greater responsibilities and wasn't content to simply let them learn from his example. He never missed an opportunity to teach. Nor would he confine his teaching to the workplace. One of his staff wrote that going to dinner with General Scott was like attending a seminar.

ADVICE

Prepare your people for advancement. While they can and should learn from your example, if that's all they do, their learning opportunities will be limited to the situations that they can observe. These are unlikely to give them the breadth of knowledge they will need to become effective leaders. Draw on your knowledge and wealth of experience to supplement their on-the-job training. Some of your best teaching can be done in relaxed, informal settings, such as over coffee or at lunch or dinner.

56. SEND A CLEAR SIGNAL

*T*HE UNITED STATES AND MEXICO SIGNED A PEACE treaty on February 2, 1848. By the terms of the treaty, the Mexicans agreed to cede their California and New Mexico territories to the United States. The treaty needed to be ratified by both the U. S. and Mexican congresses.

The U. S. Congress was embroiled in a debate over whether slavery would be permitted in the conquered territories, and the Senate was moving slowly on ratification. Meanwhile some political leaders were calling the war unjust and demanding that the United States take no territory from Mexico. This caused Lee to write:

It would be curious now if we should refuse to accept the territory we have forced her to relinquish and fight her three years more to compel her to take it back. It would be marvelously like us.

The Mexican Congress also needed to ratify the treaty, and Lee was concerned that

the discussions in [the U.S.] Congress and speeches of some of our leading men are calculated to so confuse the public mind here [in Mexico] that it may encourage them to delay and procrastinate.

ADVICE

Make sure your negotiating team is presenting a united front. You can't negotiate effectively if you are sending mixed messages. The other side will delay coming to terms while it seeks to exploit your internal dissension to its own advantage.

57. HAVE THE DEBATE FIRST

*F*ROM LEE'S PERSPECTIVE, THE PROBLEM WITH THE debates about the origin and justification of the war was that they should have occurred before the war started.

It is rather late in the day to discuss the origin of the war; that ought to have been understood before we engaged in it.

If we have been wrong in our course, we should have discovered it before.

ADVICE

Before you begin any project, have a healthy and vigorous debate about the reasons for doing the project in the first place, the methods and procedures that will and won't be followed in carrying it out, the expected results upon completion, and the milestones that will be used to measure progress.

58. DON'T CHANGE HORSES IN MIDSTREAM

*N*ICHOLAS P. TRIST WAS THE UNITED STATES HIGH Commissioner in Mexico. He had negotiated the peace treaty, which was favorable to the United States, and he had earned the respect and trust of the Mexican negotiators. Before the treaty was ratified, Trist was replaced by a new commissioner. Lee feared that

> *this hot dispatch of envoys will cause the Mexicans to believe that we are overanxious to accept their terms, and that they will be coy . . . to ratify on their part. They are very shrewd, and it will be difficult to get them to act before trying the strength of the new commissioner and making an effort for a mitigation of terms.*

A D V I C E

Don't change your team in the middle of a delicate negotiation. The other side will question your motives, and your new negotiators will lose time establishing their credibility. The only exceptions to this rule should be for death or serious illness, or if your negotiators are clearly failing, and you need to make a fresh start.

59. BE FAIR BUT FIRM

*L*EE WAS FRUSTRATED BY WHAT HE VIEWED AS MEXICAN intransigence toward ratifying the treaty.

I would not exact now more than I would have taken before the commencement of hostilities, as I should wish for nothing, but what was just.

In my humble opinion it would have been better to . . . submit it [the treaty] to the Mexican Government, and if within the prescribed time they thought proper to ratify it to . . . march the army home; but if not to tear up the paper and . . . take the country up to . . . whatever other southern boundary they [the U. S. government] should think proper for the United States. I think we might reasonably expect that they [the Mexicans] would lose no time in ratifying the present treaty. I might make a rough diplomatist, but a tolerably quick one.

A D V I C E

If you are fair and firm, your negotiations should lead to fruitful results. Be careful the other party doesn't misconstrue your attempt to be fair for weakness, because then you would need to demonstrate your willingness to hold firm, even if that means getting involved in a lengthy and expensive controversy or lawsuit.

60. LET OTHERS SING YOUR PRAISES

*L*EE HAD PERFORMED BRILLIANTLY IN MEXICO, BUT YOU wouldn't be able to tell that from him. In response to praise from his brother, Smith, he wrote:

As to myself, your brotherly feelings have made you estimate too highly my small services, and though praise from one I love so dearly is sweet, truth compels me to disclaim it. I did nothing more than what others in my place would have done much better.

ADVICE

If you have to blow your own horn to get noticed, you're in the wrong organization. Go someplace else, where merit is recognized and rewarded. On the other hand, if you are working where good performance is noticed, and you still are trumpeting your own successes, stop it. It's unnecessary and counterproductive, and indicates such insecurity on your part as to raise legitimate questions about your fitness for promotion.

4

PREPARE
YOURSELF

June 1848–March 1855

Lee's first assignment after the Mexican War is to supervise the construction of Fort Carroll, near Baltimore, Maryland. In 1852, he is appointed Superintendent of the U.S. Military Academy. Lee takes advantage of the opportunity West Point affords to continue his military studies. Regarding Lee's fitness for command, General Winfield Scott says, "I tell you, that if I were on my death-bed tomorrow, and the President of the United States should tell me that a great battle was to be fought for the liberty or slavery of the country, and asked my judgment as to the ability of a commander, I would say with my dying breath, 'Let it be Robert E. Lee.'"

61. THE BUDGET GAME

*A*FTER RETURNING FROM MEXICO IN JUNE 1848, LEE was assigned to oversee the construction of a new fort (Fort Carroll) for the defense of Baltimore. Of the initial appropriation for its construction, there was a balance of $36,000 when Lee filed his annual report on September 1, 1849. He requested and received an additional $50,000 for the coming fiscal year. When Lee filed his report the following year, the balance had increased to $68,000. Stating that he planned to spend all of that by the end of June 1851, Lee requested another $50,000. Congress adjourned without approving the additional appropriation, so there was concern that the work would have to stop. But on September 30, 1852, Lee reported that he still had $41,000 in unspent funds, enough to continue construction for nearly another year.

ADVICE

In too many organizations, budgeting is a game. Managers ask for more money than they need, knowing that their budgets will be cut. Senior executives cut budgets arbitrarily because they know that the requested budgets are inflated. The budget review process becomes an exercise to determine which managers can tell the most believable lies. When the year is over, some companies award bonuses based on performance against goals, such as service levels and project deliverables, and largely ignore budgetary performance. Others focus on results against budget and pay little attention to the deterioration in performance that irrational budget cutting may have caused.

˵ Insist that your people prepare realistic budgets and then manage to them. Establish a plus-and-minus tolerance for each budget based on the level of risk and uncertainty associated with the work to be accomplished. Then, putting extraordinary circumstances aside, treat managers who come in significantly under budget the same as you treat those who come in significantly over budget.

62. CONFLICT OF INTEREST

*W*HILE LEE WAS BUSY CONSTRUCTING FORT CARROLL, some Cuban revolutionaries living in exile were planning to invade Cuba and win independence from Spain. They asked Lee to take command of their army and made him an extremely attractive monetary offer. Lee went to Washington to seek the advice of Senator Jefferson Davis, who was Chairman of the Military Affairs Committee. Davis recalled

> *that the point on which he [Lee] wished particularly to consult me was as to the propriety of entertaining the proposition which had been made to him. He had been educated in the service of the United States, and felt it wrong to accept service in the army of a foreign power while he held his commission.*

In the end, Lee declined the Cubans' offer.

ADVICE

When one of your company's competitors makes you a lucrative offer, ask yourself how much loyalty you owe to your current employer. It would be unethical to take the secrets that are locked in your desk to a new company, but what about the secrets in your head? You can't avoid taking those with you. Lee wrote, "I hold to the belief that you must act right whatever the consequences." Only you can decide whether it's right to go to work for one of your current competitors.

Companies do try to protect themselves through the use of non-compete agreements, but these tend to be ineffective or unenforceable. They work best in those cases where the company continues to provide benefits and compensation to the former employee, since these can be eliminated if the provisions of the non-compete agreement are violated. Otherwise, the company has little leverage. The only defense is to try to hire people with integrity and then provide them with challenging work and satisfactory compensation.

63. BE IN NO ONE'S DEBT

*L*EE'S SON, CUSTIS, HAD ENTERED WEST POINT IN JULY 1850. The following May, liquor was found in Custis' room. This was an offense punishable by expulsion. Custis denied that he had brought alcohol on campus and said he didn't know how it had gotten into his room. It was the tradition at the U.S. Military Academy that if a cadet's classmates took a pledge that for a year they would not commit the same offense of which he stood accused, then he would not be expelled. Custis refused to accept their pledge, and Lee supported him in that decision.

I am fond of independence. . . . I wish neither to seek or receive indulgence from any one.

ADVICE

The fewer favors you owe, the better off you are. Don't allow yourself to be put into the position of feeling you need to take an action, such as promoting the wrong person or not letting a contract to the most qualified bidder because you are beholden to someone.

Custis was not dismissed. He went on to graduate first in his class.

64. PHYSICAL COMFORT

ON SEPTEMBER 1, 1852, LEE BECAME THE NINTH superintendent of the United States Military Academy at West Point. He accepted the position reluctantly because he knew

the character of cadets well enough to be convinced that it is no easy matter to make the labor of mind and body pleasant to them.

Lee recommended a number of improvements to the Academy's physical plant: a new riding hall and a new wharf, stables to shelter the horses, additions to the hospital and the officers' quarters, and improvements to the roads and water supply. He even tried to replace the cap worn by the cadets because it was

heavy, harsh and uncomfortable to the head. The black patent leather crown when exposed to the hot sun in summer is particularly objectionable, causing headache, dizziness, etc.

ADVICE

Some managers, perhaps to emphasize how lean and mean their organizations are, seem to delight in cramming their people into crowded, uncomfortable facilities, such as telephone centers that are so noisy that it's almost impossible to hear the customer. It may be necessary to work under adverse conditions in the field, but it should not be necessary in the office, dorm or classroom. You don't have to provide a palace for your people, but they can't do their best work if physically uncomfortable. Similarly don't ask your uniformed workers to wear outfits that impede their ability to do their jobs.

65. THE WORKING MANAGER FALLACY

*W*HEN LEE BECAME SUPERINTENDENT, THE ACADEMY'S department heads taught classes in addition to administering their departments. This left them little time to monitor the performance of their staff or work on improving the curriculum. One of the measures Lee took to raise West Point's academic standards was to release department heads from their teaching duties.

ADVICE

In a misguided attempt to save money, some organizations promote promising performers to "working managers." The fallacy is that a manager really does have work to do, and there isn't enough time or energy to do all of the management work and still do the work he or she was doing before being promoted. Your people won't succeed as managers if you bury them in non-management work.

66. DON'T ENCOURAGE SNITCHES

$\mathcal{O}$NE DAY WHILE RIDING WITH HIS YOUNGEST SON, ROB, Lee spotted three cadets who were off campus, a serious offense. As his son recalled, the cadets

> *immediately leaped over a low wall on the side of the road and disappeared from our view. We rode on for a moment in silence; then my father said: "Did you know those young men? But no; if you did, don't say so."*

A D V I C E

Don't encourage your people to come bearing tales about minor infractions. When employees rat on one another, the work environment turns sour.

67. MAKE IT EASIER TO DO RIGHT

*A*FTER SEEING THE OFF-LIMITS CADETS, LEE SAID TO his son:

I wish boys would do what is right, it would be so much easier for all parties.

When Lee became Superintendent, cadets could accumulate two hundred demerits in a single academic year before being subject to dismissal. To make it easier for cadets to do what was right, Lee changed the cut-off for dismissal to one hundred demerits in six months. Cadets could no longer afford to wait until they had a large number of demerits before paying attention to the rules governing their conduct. As a result, the number of cadets with a "deficiency in conduct" sufficient to warrant their dismissal was reduced.

ADVICE

The annual performance appraisal is an American corporate standard, but performance is far too important a subject to be discussed only annually. There are usually procedures for putting those who are clearly failing on probation and for closely monitoring their performance. Star performers are noticed and receive recognition and rewards. Average performers frequently fall through the cracks. The only time their work is reviewed is when they have their annual performance appraisal. Identifying opportunities for improving performance and revising goals accordingly should ideally be a continuous process, but as a practical matter, most managers don't have the time. Six-month reviews are an important step toward helping your people "do what is right."

68. GIVE THEM A GRACEFUL WAY OUT

*W*HEN A CADET HAD FAILING MARKS AND WAS GOING TO have to be dismissed, Lee would offer him the opportunity to resign. To the father of one such cadet, Lee wrote:

He is a youth of such fine feelings and good character that I should not like to subject him to the mortification of failure, to which he might give more value than it deserves. For I consider the character of no man affected by want of success provided he has made an honest effort to succeed.

ADVICE

If some of your people are giving it their best effort but just don't have what it takes to make it in the job they're in, let them out gracefully. Help them to find other jobs within the organization for which they are better suited, or failing that, give them the opportunity to resign.

69. IF THEY DON'T CARE

*T*HERE WERE CADETS THAT LEE DID NEED TO DISMISS from the Academy. In one case, the cadet not only had poor grades, he also had a smart mouth. When asked how he would feel if during a dinner conversation his lack of knowledge about an important battle became apparent, he answered:

Why, I should refuse to associate with people who would talk of such things at dinner.

He was also a disciplinary problem. Asked to explain his absence from the parade ground, he replied:

If I was absent without your knowledge or permission, sir, how did you know I was absent.

Finally, after failing his chemistry exam, the cadet was dismissed from the Academy. He appealed his dismissal. Lee reviewed his record and gave him every benefit of the doubt, expunging twenty-five of the demerits he had accumulated, but even that was not enough. He still had twenty-one more demerits than the cut-off for dismissal.

I can therefore do nothing more in his behalf, nor do I know of anything entitling him to further indulgence—I can only regret that one so capable of doing well should so have neglected himself, and must now suffer the penalty.

ADVICE

You can't help someone succeed who isn't willing to make the effort. People who don't care about the job they're doing don't deserve to have that job. Termination may give them the impetus to find a job that they will care about.

The cadet, James McNeill Whistler, who had been first in his class in drawing, went on to become a famous artist.

70. YOU CAN ONLY CARE SO MUCH

*L*EE FELT PERSONALLY RESPONSIBLE FOR EACH CADET. He wrote that having to dismiss any of them was "the most unpleasant office I am called on to perform." After Jefferson Davis became Secretary of War in 1853, he visited Lee at West Point. Davis was surprised to see how gray Lee's hair had turned. As Davis recalled, Lee

confessed that the cadets did exceedingly worry him, and then it was perceptible that his sympathy with young people was rather an impediment than a qualification for the superintendency.

ADVICE

You can only bear so much responsibility for the failures of others. The bulk of it must lie on their shoulders, not yours.

71. LEARNING AND UNDERSTANDING

*O*NE OF LEE'S WORRIES WAS THAT CADETS WERE ABLE TO pass their examinations without really understanding what they had learned.

Cadets deceive themselves sometimes by thinking they study, when in reality they do not, and are satisfied by reading over or devoting reasonable time with their lessons. You know the difference between that and understanding.

A D V I C E

If your people learn without understanding the rationale underlying the material you are teaching, you will have done no more than teach parrots to talk. In too many companies, the managers can rattle off mission, vision and quality statements, but they can't tell you how they relate to their job. Never equate learning and understanding; they are not synonyms in real life.

72. MANAGEMENT TRAINEES

*L*EE RECOGNIZED THAT CADETS COULD "NEITHER BE treated as school boys or soldiers."

These young gentlemen are not considered exactly in the light of enlisted men, and as much deference as possible is paid their convenience and wishes in relation to personal matters.

ADVICE

Management trainees present a unique problem. Those that are hired directly out of college with no relevant work experience first need to learn the jobs that they will later be expected to supervise. Some experienced managers, because they either fear competition or have a visceral dislike for wunderkind, do everything they can to sabotage the trainees. Others handle management trainees with kid gloves, and their charges move into management positions without having first learned the business. Effective management trainee programs combine formal study with on-the-job training under the overall supervision of an independent review board that is responsible for assessing each trainee's progress.

73. IT'S A WORKPLACE, NOT A PRISON

*C*ADETS WOULD OCCASIONALLY SNEAK OFF CAMPUS AND head for the local taverns. Drinking and being absent without leave were serious breaches of discipline, but Lee was unwilling to take stringent security measures that, for all practical purposes, would have turned West Point into a prison.

Young men must not expect to escape contact with evil, but must learn not to be contaminated by it. That virtue is worth but little that requires constant watching and removal from temptation.

ADVICE

You need to protect the organization against fraud and abuse, but turning the workplace into a virtual prison is counterproductive. A balance needs to be struck between treating your employees like children who will behave badly if not constantly watched, and assuming that everyone is honest and trustworthy. Sensible security procedures supplemented by a strong internal audit arm are your best defense.

74. DISCIPLINE

*L*EE DID NOT ENJOY DISCIPLINING WAYWARD CADETS, but he believed

> *when it is necessary, true kindness requires it should be applied with a firm hand.*

A D V I C E

Many managers shy away from taking disciplinary measures because they are so distasteful. When finally forced to take action by repeated offenses, they take less severe action than called for. Such misguided efforts to be kind invariably backfire, and the situation spirals out of control until termination becomes the only remedy. Discipline should be used sparingly, but when necessary, it should be applied consistently and firmly.

75. TAKE VACATION

*L*EE FELT THAT VACATIONS WERE VALUABLE AND beneficial. He thought that a summer holiday for the cadets was

> *a benefit. It is a great gratification. Its prospect holds out encouragement to better behavior; and its enjoyment has a tendency to enlarge their ideas, ameliorate many contracted notions, and renders them more happy and contented during the rest of the course.*

ADVICE

Don't fall into the trap of thinking that the organization will suffer irreparable harm if you or someone working for you takes a vacation. Vacations are important to rejuvenate body and mind. After a vacation, people come back to work re-energized. Encourage your people to take vacations. One way to do that is to not pay them for unused vacation days.

76. PERSONAL LEAVE

*L*EE BELIEVED IN TAKING VACATION, BUT HE WAS reluctant to grant leave for special occasions.

The cadets are placed here for a particular object, and if the indulgence in question is granted to one, it must be extended to all. You therefore see it would materially interfere with their course of studies and instruction.

I think it would be unjust to his class . . . to grant him a leave of absence equally desirable to them all.

ADVICE

Some organizations prescribe strict rules for the granting of personal leave: five days for the death of a parent, two days for the death of an aunt or uncle. Inevitably, this causes their employees to ask for exceptions. Others provide unlimited personal leave subject to manager approval. This puts the monkey on the backs of their managers, who are placed in the impossible position of trying to play God. Do you give the same amount of time off to attend a wedding in New Delhi as you do for one in Omaha? Does the death of a close uncle warrant the same number of days of personal leave as that of . . . ? The best thing to do is to provide your people with sufficient personal leave to handle normal contingencies, and then let them decide how to use it. When necessary, they can use or even borrow annual vacation days to meet an extraordinary need.

77. CRITICAL POSITIONS

*T*he hospital at West Point had two doctors. On one occasion, when one of the doctors was away, the other became ill, leaving no one to care for the patients. After some delay and not without some difficulty, Lee was able to get a doctor from New York City to take over temporarily. Lee knew he was lucky that none of the hospitalized cadets had died while the Academy had been without an attending physician.

ADVICE

Critical positions must never be left unfilled. If you only have two people who can do a specific critical task, and one of them is going on leave, make arrangements in advance to cover for the other one in the event of an emergency. This may require calling on a contractor, a former employee, or someone who previously held that position and has since transferred within the organization.

78. AT EASE

O N SATURDAYS, LEE WOULD INVITE A NUMBER OF CADETS to his home for tea or supper. As Lee's son, Rob, recalled:

> *The misery of some of these lads, owing to embarrassment, possibly from awe of the Superintendent, was pitiable and evident even to me, a boy of ten or eleven years old. But as soon as my father got command, as it were, of the situation, one could see how quickly most of them were put at their ease. He would address himself to the task of making them feel comfortable and at home, and his genial manner and pleasant ways at once succeeded.*

Lee was obviously successful in his efforts to set the boys at ease because there were always a number of cadets that showed up uninvited. Lee expressed surprise at this, saying that he would have thought that the cadets would find

> *the Superintendent and his dame dull commodities in the interchange of social pleasure.*

A D V I C E

Some senior executives seem to enjoy lording it over their subordinates at social events. They like being held in awe, and use their position to intimidate others even in off-the-job situations. Good leaders, however, take off their epaulets and make their people feel comfortable and at ease.

One cadet, who was a frequent Saturday visitor, wrote to his mother that Lee was the "handsomest man . . . just like a marble model." His mother responded, "Handsome, yes, but not like marble. Colonel Lee is very human, kind, calm and definite. The cadets are fortunate to have a superintendent to whom they can look up to with whole hearted admiration and respect—That means a great deal to youth."

79. TEACH, DON'T PREACH

ON SUNDAYS, LEE AND HIS FAMILY ATTENDED CHURCH. As his son, Rob, recalled, Lee was never

late for Sunday service at the Post Chapel. . . . There he sat very straight—well up the middle aisle—and, as I remember, always became very sleepy, and sometimes even took a little nap during the sermon.

The chaplain at West Point used his pulpit to harangue the cadets. According to Lee's daughter, Agnes, he was "a little hard on the cadets and too pointed in his remarks." His sermons must have lulled Lee to sleep.

ADVICE

Long, repetitious harangues and lectures are boring and turn people off. So does yelling. They are ineffective as teaching tools because people who have tuned you out can't learn anything from you. If you make a habit of speaking softly and saying it only once, people will listen and learn.

80. DO IT CHEERFULLY OR RESIGN

*L*EE DID NOT ENJOY BEING AT WEST POINT. HE TOLD A friend that he would relinquish the Superintendent's post "with more cheerfulness than I felt reluctance in undertaking it." However, when asked if he was dissatisfied, he replied:

> I am not dissatisfied. Nor has any soldier cause to be while endeavoring to perform his duty. That duty may [be] . . . distasteful and impalatable, but while assigned to its performance, he has no right to be dissatisfied, much less express it. . . . I have more at heart the prosperity of the Academy than my own pleasure, while under my charge I shall administer it to the best of my ability.

ADVICE

If you don't like your job, you have the right to find another. What you shouldn't do is publicly gripe and moan because that can impact the attitude and performance of your co-workers.

Lee believed, "You must expect discomforts and annoyances all through life. No place is secure from them, and you must make up your mind to meet with them and bear them."

81. EXERCISE

$\mathcal{O}$NE UNION GENERAL, REMEMBERING HIS PRE-CIVIL WAR association with Lee, wrote that he was

> *then in the vigor of youthful strength, with a noble and commanding presence, and an admirable, graceful, and athletic figure.*

Lee's work as an engineer frequently had to be done outdoors and often under adverse conditions. He thrived on strenuous physical activity. While in Mexico, Lee wrote that there were "few men more hearty or more able to bear exposure and fatigue" than he. One reason Lee didn't enjoy his West Point assignment was that his duties required him to spend long days in his office, and he hated being tied down to a desk. Lee believed that this sedentary life was ruining his health. He suffered from indigestion and felt rundown.

ADVICE

Exercise may be as important to mental health as it is to physical well-being. The physical fitness of your employees has a direct bearing on your organization's productivity. Take steps, like providing workout facilities or defraying the cost of gym memberships, to encourage your people to exercise and be physically active.

82. PREPARE YOURSELF

*L*EE TOOK ADVANTAGE OF HIS TIME AT WEST POINT TO continue his military education. He carefully studied Caesar and Napoleon's campaigns and writings on the art of war. He borrowed a map of Turkey to trace the movements in the Crimean War which was going on at the time. Lee also discussed military topics with members of the faculty and other distinguished army officers, including General Winfield Scott.

Engineering officers did not command troops in the field, and Lee had spent his entire army career in the Corps of Engineers, but he used his time at West Point to help prepare himself for a field command.

ADVICE

No one starts out as a general manager. Your people, including their managers, work at specialized tasks. People in staff positions, who have made the effort to learn all the facets of the business, deserve the promotional opportunities that arise outside their area of specialization. So do line managers who become computer literate and learn management accounting. They are your future general managers.

In a letter to his daughter, Mildred, Lee wrote: "You say rightly, the more you learn the more you are conscious of your ignorance. Because the more you know, the more you find there is to know in this grand and beautiful world. It is only the ignorant who suppose themselves omniscient. You will find all the days of your life that there is much to learn and much to do."

83. MAKE PARTING A SWEET SORROW

*O*N MARCH 3, 1855, LEE WAS PROMOTED TO THE permanent rank of lieutenant colonel and named deputy commander of a cavalry regiment.* Lee had spent nearly twenty-six years in the Corps of Engineers. As he prepared to transfer to the cavalry, he wrote to the Chief Engineer:

> *In thus severing my connection with the Corps of Engineers, I cannot express the pain I feel in parting from its Officers, or my grateful sense of your constant kindness and consideration. My best exertions have been devoted to its service, and my warmest feelings will be cherished for its memory.*

ADVICE

Changing jobs should be a dignified process. Don't use the move as an opportunity to reopen old wounds and replay past grievances. If you are making the change, this is not the time to tell your old boss what you don't like. If one of your people is leaving, don't recite a litany of his or her faults. Remember, you can't re-cross a burned bridge. Make your parting, in Shakespeare's words, a "sweet sorrow."

---

*While Lee had received a temporary promotion to colonel during the Mexican War, he had continued to hold the permanent grade of captain.

TAKE COMMAND

March 1855–March 1861

*Lee gains valuable experience commanding cavalry.
On leave at home in Arlington, Lee is ordered to take
command of troops being assembled to put down a
rumored insurrection at the U.S. armory and arsenal at
Harpers Ferry, Virginia. Leading troops in combat for
the first time in his thirty-year army career, Lee acts
quickly and decisively. The leader of the raid, John
Brown, is captured, and subsequently tried and hanged.
While Lee surmises that the plan to incite a slave revolt
"was the attempt of a fanatic or a madman," northern
abolitionists are successful in portraying John Brown's
execution as martyrdom. Southern reaction is
predictable, causing one newspaper to comment, "The
Harpers Ferry invasion has advanced the cause of
disunion more than any event that has happened since
the formation of the government."*

84. CLEANLINESS IS NEXT TO GODLINESS

IN JULY 1855, LEE'S REGIMENT WAS STATIONED AT Jefferson Barracks, near St. Louis, Missouri.

I have been busy all the week superintending and drilling recruits. Not a stitch of clothing has as yet arrived for them, though I made the necessary requisition for it to be sent here more than two months ago in Louisville. Yesterday, at muster, I found one of the late arrivals in a dirty, tattered shirt and pants. . . . I asked him why he did not put on clean clothes. He said he had none. I asked him if he could not wash and mend those. He said he had nothing else to put on. I then told him immediately after muster to go down to the river, wash his clothes, and sit on the bank and watch the passing steamboats till they dried, and then mend them. This morning at inspection he looked as proud as possible, stood in the position of a soldier with his little fingers on the seams of his pants . . . and his toes sticking through his shoes, but his skin and solitary two garments clean. He grinned very happily at my compliments.

ADVICE

People don't need to wear suits to take pride in their appearance, but people who don't take pride in their appearance often don't take pride in their work.

85. FAT CATS

$\mathcal{I}$N APRIL 1856, LEE TOOK COMMAND OF CAMP COOPER, which was located on a Comanche Indian reservation some 250 miles north-northwest of San Antonio, Texas. Lee told his daughter, Agnes, that he had wanted to bring a cat to Camp Cooper and had seen three suitable candidates, but his first two choices were not available and his third choice died.

I foretold his end. Coffee and cream for breakfast. Pound cake for lunch. Turtle and oysters for dinner. Buttered toast for tea, and Mexican rats, taken raw, for supper! Cat nature could not stand so much luxury. He grew enormously and ended in a spasm. His beauty could not save him.

ADVICE

While written to amuse his daughter, Lee's story of the untimely end of the fat cat is a useful parable. Some executives act as though the exertion of climbing to the top of the corporate ladder entitles them to outlandish luxuries. A powerful and independent audit committee of the board of directors can help remind them of what they sometimes forget. They are in positions of corporate trust and must not abuse their power or allow their indulgences to make them lethargic or distract them from their duties.

Lee did have a pet rattlesnake at Camp Cooper. He also kept chickens in a coop that protected them from predators, "but furnishes little protection against rain. Soldier hens . . . must learn not to mind rain."

86. GROUND RULES

*T*HERE WERE APPROXIMATELY FIVE HUNDRED Comanches living on the reservation. Shortly after taking command, Lee told their chief, Catumseh how he expected them to behave.

I hailed him as a friend as long as his conduct and that of his tribe deserved it, but would meet him as an enemy the first moment he failed to keep his word.

ADVICE

When doing business with someone for the first time, clearly state your expectations. By doing so, you will avoid future misunderstandings that could prove costly.

87. LOCAL CUSTOMS

ONE OF THE COMANCHE CHIEFS BECAME ILL, AND LEE was asked to visit him. However, when he arrived at the chief's lodge, he was not warmly greeted.

The medicine man rushed at me, made significant signs that I must disrobe before presenting myself before the august patient. I patiently sat on my horse till I ascertained what garment they considered most inimical to the practice of the healing art, which I learned to be the cravat. Then alighting, unbuttoning my coat and slipping off the noxious article, I displayed to their admiring eyes a blue check shirt, and was greeted by a general approving humph.

ADVICE

You will do business far more successfully if you learn and show respect for the local customs of the people you are dealing with.

88. WHEN YOU HOLD THEM IN CONTEMPT

*L*EE HAD A VERY LOW OPINION OF THE COMANCHE.

Their paint and ornaments make them more hideous than nature made them and the whole race is extremely uninteresting.

These people give a world of trouble to man and horse, and . . . they are not worth it.

Except when his duties required it, Lee had no contact with the Comanches, and even at that, he saw "more of them than I desire." In June 1856, he led an expedition against a band of Comanches who were raiding settlements. They led him on a merry chase that "traversed 1600 miles of the most barren and least inviting country I have ever seen." Lee learned the hard way that he had greatly underestimated the intelligence and skill of his opponents. After forty days of searching for hostile Indians, he had almost nothing to show for his efforts. His force had killed two men and captured one woman. Lee considered the expedition a failure: "We lost no men . . . but were not compensated for our labors."

ADVICE

If you are contemptuous of your competitors, you will probably be so blinded by your feelings that you will fail to recognize what they do well and what you can learn from them.

89. FIGHTING IS EASIER

*L*EE BELIEVED THAT "FIGHTING IS THE EASIEST PART OF a soldier's duty."

> *It is the watching, waiting, laboring, starving, freezing, wilting, exposure and privations that is so wearing to the body and trying to the mind. It is in this state that discipline tells; and attention night and day on the part of the officer so necessary. His eye and thoughts must be continually on his men. Their wants anticipated and comforts provided.*

ADVICE

Normally when we think of good managers, we picture them in hectic times dealing with crises or rapidly changing conditions. What makes these managers successful when the going gets tough is that they were tough when the going was easy. By staying focused and disciplined and making sure their people are properly trained and equipped, they are able to bring their units to maximum performance rapidly when required.

90. HASTY JUDGMENTS

*L*EE HAD A REPUTATION FOR BEING SCRUPULOUSLY FAIR. As one officer who knew him in Texas wrote:

He examined everything thoroughly and continuously, until master of every detail, ever too conscientious to act under imperfect knowledge of any subject submitted to him.

On one occasion, seeing that the soldier who had been brought before him on charges was nervous, Lee sought to reassure him by saying, "You shall have justice." To which the man replied, "That is what I am afraid of, sir."

ADVICE

Don't make hasty judgments. Develop a reputation for thoroughly reviewing the facts before coming to any conclusions. This is especially important in deciding cases where disciplinary action may be necessary.

91. MERGERS

*W*HEN ONE OF HIS JUNIOR OFFICERS ASKED HIS ADVICE on the subject of marriage, Lee told him:

Never marry unless you can do so into a family that will enable your children to feel proud of both sides of the house.

ADVICE

Lee's advice on marriage applies to any contemplated merger. Don't do the deal, unless both organizations are going to benefit, and not just financially. The key people need to feel good about getting in bed together.

THERE'S MORE THAN ONE WAY TO SKIN A CAT.
In 1839, Robert E. Lee was supervising the construction of improvements on the Mississippi River. When a land developer obtained an injunction that prevented the Corps of Engineers from continuing to build the dikes that had been planned, Lee loaned his equipment to the City of St. Louis so the work could continue under the direction of his civilian assistant.
(Library of Congress)

DON'T GIVE THEM A BEACHHEAD. The U. S. Army landed at Vera Cruz on March 9, 1847. Instead of opposing the landing when the Americans were most vulnerable, the Mexicans chose to remain behind the city's walls. After a short siege, Vera Cruz surrendered.
(Library of Congress)

HISTORY IS THE BEST TEACHER.

American soldiers captured the fortress of Chapultepec on September 13, 1847. The victory was costly because in August General Winfield Scott had granted the Mexicans an armistice, the terms of which they violated by reinforcing their defenses. Scott had failed to learn from the experience of General Zachary Taylor who the year before had suffered the same fate.

(Library of Congress)

DISCIPLINE.

Lee was the Superintendent of the United States Military Academy at West Point from September 1852 to March 1855. He disliked having to discipline cadets, but he believed that when it was necessary "true kindness requires it should be applied with a firm hand."

(Library of Congress)

PREPARE YOURSELF. This West Point building housed Lee's office and the library, which he used to prepare himself for possible future assignments.

(National Archives)

WHEN YOU HOLD THEM IN CONTEMPT. Commanding cavalry in Texas in 1856, Lee had a low opinion of Comanche Indians. However, when a marauding band led him on a 1,600 mile merry goose chase, he realized that he had underestimated his opponents.

(National Archives)

AT ALL TIMES READY. On October 18, 1859, U. S. Marines under the command of Robert E. Lee stormed the firehouse at Harpers Ferry putting an end to John Brown's raid. In his report, Lee commended "the conduct of the detachment of Marines, who were at all times ready and prompt in the execution of any duty."

(Marine Corps University Foundation)

HOBSON'S CHOICE. On April 14, 1861, after a 33 hour bombardment, the Confederate flag was raised over Fort Sumter. Instead of considering all the possible options, Jefferson Davis had focused on only two. Do nothing, in which case the fragile Confederacy would dissolve, or attack the fort and start a war that the Confederacy would probably lose.

(National Archives)

DO THE WORK OF THE DAY. Lee's favorite relaxation was to ride his beloved Traveller. He was able to relax at the end of each day because, as one aide recalled, his working style was so disciplined that "at the close of his office hours every matter requiring prompt attention had been disposed of."
(Library of Congress)

PARADIGM SHIFTING TECHNOLOGY. When it was completed in 1847, Fort Pulaski, built for the defense of Savannah, was thought to be as impregnable as Gibraltar. In April 1862, Union artillery, using new weaponry, took only two days to pound the fort into submission.
(U. S. Army Military History Institute)

COME AND JOIN US BROTHERS.
PUBLISHED BY THE SUPERVISORY COMMITTEE FOR RECRUITING COLORED REGIMENTS
1210 CHESTNUT ST. PHILADELPHIA.

HALF MEASURES. Lee believed that total mobilization, including the use of black soldiers, was required for the Confederacy to win the war. The Confederate Congress waited too long to act, and then only partially adopted Lee's recommendations. The Union recruited 180,000 African-Americans into its armies, over 130,000 of them from Southern states.

(Library of Congress)

BLUFF. "Quaker guns" were used to deceive Union commanders into overestimating the strength of Confederate fortifications.

(Library of Congress)

ON LOCATING THE OFFICE. The defense of Richmond became a paramount consideration after it became the Confederate capital in 1861. Lee believed that "Richmond was the millstone that was dragging down the army." This photograph of Richmond was taken in April 1865. A fire set by the evacuating Confederates to destroy war materials burned out of control and destroyed one-third of the city.

(National Archives)

EARN THEIR RESPECT. After replacing the wounded Joseph E. Johnston as the commander of the Army of Northern Virginia, Lee set out to earn the respect of his men. By war's end, he had become one of the most admired, respected and beloved military leaders in history.

(Library of Congress)

THE WINNING IMAGE. General Robert E. Lee.

(Library of Congress)

92. TALK IS CHEAP, UNTIL YOU HIRE A LAWYER

*L*EE WAS FREQUENTLY DETAILED TO COURT-MARTIAL duty. In one case, the defendant was represented by two lawyers who were, according to Lee,

> *very shrewd men, accustomed to the tricks and strata-gems of special pleadings, which if of no other avail, absorb time and stave off questions.*

ADVICE

If you are going to get involved in litigation, remember having the facts on your side is, unfortunately, not nearly as important as having good lawyers. Avoid the legal system, if possible. If you are forced into a legal battle, don't expect a quick or easy victory. Lawyers rarely use the word "justice." They talk about cost instead. Be prepared to spend outrageous sums of money and be dragged through seemingly endless years of legal maneuvering.

93. COMRADESHIP

IN OCTOBER 1857, LEE LEARNED THAT HIS FATHER-IN-LAW had died. He immediately applied for leave to return home. To his commanding officer, he confided:

I can see that I have at last to decide the question, which I have staved off for 20 years. Whether I am to continue in the army all my life or to leave it.

While Lee thought about becoming a farmer, he was reluctant to resign his commission because of "the cordiality and friendship in the army."

It is that I believe that has kept me in it so long, and it is that which makes me now fear to leave it. I do not know where I should meet with so much friendship out of it.

ADVICE

A congenial work environment is a powerful retention tool. People that enjoy working in an organization tend not to look for other jobs. They have to be recruited away at substantially higher salaries, and even then are reluctant to leave.

*L*EE RETURNED TO ARLINGTON IN NOVEMBER 1857.
Except for court-martial duty and an occasional special
assignment, he remained on leave for over two years. A. L.
Long, who served on Lee's staff during the Civil War,
recalled an incident from this period:

> *Colonel Lee came to Mr. Schneider [a blacksmith] to
> have made a peculiar gate-latch [Lee had designed] that
> could be opened without dismounting. He wanted a dozen,
> and Mr. Schneider said, "Well, colonel, I will make one. If
> that pleases you, I will make eleven more."*

ADVICE

No matter how promising a new product looks, pilot test it
before going into production.

95. TAKE ALL THE TIME YOU CAN

*S*TILL TRYING TO DECIDE WHETHER TO RESIGN FROM THE army, Lee wrote:

> *As to myself and future plans, I shall defer my deter-mination until the fall, as it will not be necessary to deter-mine till then.*

ADVICE

When asked to make a decision, the best managers always ask the question: Is this a decision that has to be made now? Make time your ally. The Roman philosopher Seneca taught, "The best remedy for anger is delay." The best way to deal with a decision is not to make it prematurely.

ON THE MORNING OF OCTOBER 17, 1859, FIRST Lieutenant James Ewell Brown (Jeb) Stuart rode out to Arlington and delivered a letter ordering Lee to report immediately to the Secretary of War. Lee rode straight to the War Department without stopping to change into his uniform. There he learned that he had been given command of the troops being assembled to put down an insurrection at the U.S. government's armory and arsenal at Harpers Ferry, Virginia.

When Lee arrived at Harpers Ferry later that night he found a chaotic scene. A small band of insurgents had seized about a dozen hostages and had taken refuge in a firehouse. There was sporadic firing between them and local residents and militia.

Lee immediately took command. He cleared the area of civilians and surrounded the firehouse. He sent word that the reinforcements being sent from Fort Monroe would not be needed. He then developed a plan to storm the firehouse.

But for fear of sacrificing the lives of some of the gentlemen held by them as prisoners in a midnight assault, I should have ordered the attack at once.

Early the next morning, he offered the rebels the opportunity to surrender. The moment they refused, the marines under his command stormed the firehouse. To minimize the risk to the hostages, the assault party used only their bayonets. Within a matter of minutes, two of the insurgents had been killed and the remaining three captured, including their leader, John Brown. None of the hostages had been harmed but two marines had been wounded, one fatally. Lee had the prisoners transported to the county jail in Charlestown, Virginia to await trial.

ADVICE

When you arrive in the middle of a confused and chaotic situation, immediately take command. Even if you aren't certain of everything that needs to be done, by decisively addressing the aspects you can deal with, you will establish your leadership presence, restore order and buy yourself the time to develop a plan to rectify the situation.

97. AVOID CREATING MARTYRS

*I*N HIS REPORT ON JOHN BROWN'S RAID, LEE WROTE, "The result proves that the plan was the attempt of a fanatic or a madman." Moderate voices in the North agreed, and when Brown was sentenced to hang, Fernando Wood, the mayor of New York, asked Virginia's governor, Henry A. Wise, to commute Brown's sentence to life imprisonment.

Have you nerve enough to send Brown to the State Prison instead of hanging him? Brown is looked upon here as the mere crazy or foolhardy emissary of other men.

These other men were preparing Brown for martyrdom. The abolitionist leader, Wendell Phillips, said:

John Brown has twice as much right to hang Governor Wise as Governor Wise has to hang him. On the banks of the Potomac, history will visit that river more kindly, because John Brown has gilded it with the eternal brightness of his glorious deed.

On the day Brown was hanged, church bells tolled and flags were lowered to half mast. Newspapers provided detailed accounts of his death and printed his final words, "I, John Brown, am now certain that the crimes of this guilty land will never be purged away, but with blood."

By not granting Brown clemency, Governor Wise had created the opportunity for the abolitionists to transform John Brown into a martyr, and they took full advantage of it.

ADVICE

You'll never face a situation as extreme as the one just described. But whenever you must discipline a subordinate, ask yourself, "Is this the minimum I can do in response to his or her errant behavior?" Never hesitate to apply discipline when necessary, but do not be heavy-handed. You don't want to create a martyr, for doing so can lead to unanticipated consequences, like giving organized labor a cause célèbre that boosts its efforts to organize your company.

98. NEPOTISM

*L*EE LEFT ARLINGTON TO RESUME ACTIVE DUTY WITH the army in Texas in February 1860. In June, Joseph E. Johnston was appointed to the post of Quartermaster General by the Secretary of War, who happened to be Johnston's cousin. While delighted at the advancement of his old friend, Lee was concerned by the preferential treatment he had received. Previously, Lee had written that

> *in proportion to his services he (Johnston) has been advanced beyond anyone in the army and has thrown more discredit than ever on the system of favoritism.*

When during the Civil War, Lee's wife suggested that he add their youngest son to his staff, he responded:

> *I am opposed to officers surrounding themselves with their sons and relatives. It is wrong in principle, and in that case the selection of officers would be made from private and social relations, rather than for the public good.*

ADVICE

No matter how talented or obviously deserving a person is of advancement, if he or she is promoted by a relative or close personal friend, the promotion will leave a sour aftertaste. Unless the organization is so small that you can't do otherwise, follow Lee's advice and give the person "an independent position where he could rise by his own merit and not through the recommendations of his relatives."

99. CONTINGENCY PLANS

In December 1860, Lee was shown a document that General Winfield Scott had written. It was entitled, "Views Suggested by the Imminent Danger, October 29, 1860, of a Disruption of the Union by the Secession of One or More of the Southern States." In it, Scott had outlined the actions that he believed should be taken to avert a civil war, or failing that, the strategy to be followed in waging one. Lee immediately said,

My friend, I must make one request of you, and that is that you will not suffer these Views to get into the newspapers.

Abraham Lincoln had been elected President of the United States, and there was widespread talk of secession throughout the South. Lee feared the publication of Scott's "Views" would add fuel to the fire, and he was correct in that assumption. When the document was printed in a Washington newspaper, it added weight to the pro-secession arguments being made by Southerners who believed that the North was planning to wage a war of aggression against the South.

ADVICE

Contingency plans are necessary, but they can be frightening when taken out of context. Their distribution must be tightly restricted to only those who need access to them.

100. BULLIES

*I*N FEBRUARY 1861, LEE RECEIVED ORDERS TO REPORT to General Scott in Washington. By this time, seven Southern states—South Carolina, Mississippi, Florida, Alabama, Georgia, Louisiana and Texas—had passed ordinances of secession. Delegates from these states had met to form a new government, and as Lee was preparing to leave Texas, Jefferson Davis took the oath of office as the first president of the Confederate States of America.

Several Texas officials met with Lee to urge him to resign his commission in the U.S. Army and join the Confederacy. They told him that unless he did so, he would not be allowed to take his personal belongings with him when he left the state. Lee refused to be intimidated and politely told them what they could do with their offer.

ADVICE

Don't be a bully. Management by intimidation is counterproductive.

Lee returned to Washington in March 1861. During that month he received an offer of a commission as a brigadier general from the Confederate Secretary of War, which he ignored. He also was promoted to the permanent rank of colonel in the U.S. Army.

6

CONFLICTING PRINCIPLES

April 1861–March 1862

Although opposed to secession, Lee feels he owes his allegiance to Virginia. When Virginia secedes, he resigns from the U.S. Army, against the advice of Winfield Scott who tells him, "You have made the greatest mistake of your life, but I feared it would be so." Appointed Virginia's commanding general, Lee mobilizes the armed forces and develops a strategic plan to defend the state. Confederate success at the first battle of Manassas (Bull Run) is due in large measure to his efforts to get Virginia ready to resist an invasion. After failing to drive Union forces from western Virginia, Lee is placed in command of the Confederacy's southeastern coastal defenses. While he calls his new assignment "another forlorn hope expedition," he is successful in strengthening the defenses of Charleston and Savannah against attack from the sea.

101. HOBSON'S CHOICE

*I*N JANUARY 1861, PRESIDENT JAMES BUCHANAN HAD authorized the resupply of Major Robert Anderson's garrison at Fort Sumter, located on an island at the entrance to the harbor of Charleston, South Carolina. The supply ship was fired upon by South Carolina militia and turned back. After Abraham Lincoln was inaugurated as President of the United States in March, he determined to reprovision the fort. Accordingly, on April 6th, he informed the Governor of South Carolina that "an attempt will be made to supply Fort Sumter with provisions only; and that, if such attempt be not resisted, no effort to throw in men, arms or ammunition, will be made."

This placed Jefferson Davis on the horns of a dilemma. Many Southerners had misgivings about secession. In Alabama, where the resolution to secede had passed by a 61–39 margin, a newspaper warned that unless Fort Sumter was taken "the people of Alabama...will be back in the old Union in less than ten days." If Davis did nothing the Confederacy might dissolve. On the other hand, attacking Fort Sumter would unite the North against the South in a civil war. A war that some influential Southerners at the time (and many historians to this day) believed the Confederacy was fated to lose. Robert Toombs, the Confederate Secretary of State, told Davis:

The firing on that fort will inaugurate a civil war greater than any the world has yet seen. . . . Mr. President, at this time it is suicide, murder, and you will lose us every friend at the North. You will wantonly strike a hornet's nest which extends from mountains to ocean. Legions now quiet will swarm out and sting us to death. It is unnecessary. It puts us in the wrong. It is fatal.

Davis chose not to heed this advice, and early on the morning of April 12, 1861, Confederate guns began firing on Fort Sumter. Three days later, Lincoln issued a call for 75,000 men. Jefferson Davis responded with a call for 100,000. The Civil War had begun.

By bombarding Fort Sumter, Jefferson Davis had succeeded in uniting the South, but he had also united the North. As Lincoln's old political foe Stephen Douglas told a pro-Union gathering, "There are only two sides to the question. Every man must be for the United States or against it. There can be no neutrals in this war, only patriots—or traitors."

Lincoln had presented Davis with a Hobson's choice. Either alternative seemed to doom the Confederacy. It is intriguing to speculate on what might have happened had Davis declined Lincoln's gambit. Instead of bombarding the fort on April 12th, he could have tried to prevent the supply ship from reaching the fort as had been done three months earlier. Major Anderson had informed the Confederates that unless resupplied he would have to evacuate the fort on April 15th. Davis might have achieved a bloodless victory, or if the Union fleet had tried to fight their way in, it might have looked like Lincoln had fired the first shot. Either way, he would have united the South, but sentiment in the North might have remained strongly divided, where many people favored letting the Southern states go in peace.

A D V I C E

Before you choose the lesser of two evils, make certain there are no other choices. Don't let how the question was framed force you into making a bad decision. Some managers faced with a competitor who has dramatically reduced prices ask themselves whether it is smarter to do nothing and lose market share or match the price cuts and lose money. Instead of focusing on the obvious two responses, they should lay out and examine all of the possible choices available to them. For example, a simple product or service enhancement might be a more cost-effective response to a competitive thrust than engaging in a price war. Your competitors expect you to accept their gambits, but you can choose to decline them, and instead of playing their game, you can make them play yours.

102. UNANTICIPATED CONSEQUENCES

ENERAL WINFIELD SCOTT HAD URGED THE EVACUATION of Fort Sumter because he feared that if war broke out, the slave-holding states that had not joined the Confederacy would also secede. He believed, "The evacuation . . . would instantly soothe and give confidence to the eight remaining slave-holding states, and render their cordial adherence to this Union perpetual."

The delegates to the Virginia convention had at the beginning of April voted against secession by a two-to-one margin. Two weeks later, in the wake of the attack on Fort Sumter and Lincoln's call for troops, they voted overwhelmingly to secede. Arkansas, Tennessee and North Carolina followed Virginia into the Confederacy.

Lincoln had hoped that by acting with firmness he would strengthen the hand of pro-union Southerners, but he realized that forcing Davis' hand could cause some additional Southern states to secede. What he did not expect was the negative reaction his call for men received from the governors of Kentucky and Missouri. The former wrote, "Kentucky will furnish no troops for the wicked purpose of subduing her sister Southern states," and the latter called Lincoln's action "illegal, unconstitutional, revolutionary, inhuman, diabolical."

Lincoln knew that the continued existence of the United States was now uncertain. As he explained:

I think to lose Kentucky is nearly the same as to lose the whole game. Kentucky gone, we cannot hold Missouri, nor, as I think, Maryland. These all against us, and the job on our hands is too large for us. We would as well consent to separation at once, including the surrender of this capital.

A D V I C E

It is rarely possible to anticipate all of the consequences that will result from an action on your part, particularly a complex one involving multiple people and organizations. But you need to try to position yourself to be able to deal effectively with any fallout.

103. ROSE-COLORED GLASSES

*D*AVIS AND LINCOLN HAD PLUNGED THE COUNTRY INTO civil war, but at what price, and to what end? Neither of them imagined a conflict that would last four years, take nearly 700,000 lives, devastate the South, and leave lasting wounds.

Lincoln had called for volunteers to serve for ninety days. In the heady euphoria that followed the attack on Fort Sumter, politicians and newspaper editors talked of a short war. Lee knew better.

Northern politicians do not appreciate the determination and pluck of the South, and Southern politicians do not appreciate the numbers, resources, and patient perseverance of the North. Both sides forget that we are all Americans, and that it must be a terrible struggle.

I foresee that the country will have to pass through a terrible ordeal, a necessary expiation, perhaps, of our national sins.

ADVICE

You can't afford to be wearing rose-colored glasses when you contemplate a risky or controversial plan. In order to be successful, you must have a realistic assessment of what you are up against.

William Tecumseh Sherman told a Southern friend, "This country will be drenched in blood, and God only knows how it will end. It is all folly, madness, a crime against civilization! You people speak so lightly of war; you don't know what you're talking about. War is a terrible thing!"

104. WHEN IT'S TOO IMPORTANT TO HOLD YOUR TONGUE

*L*EE WAS OPPOSED TO SECESSION. HE COULD "ANTICIPATE no greater calamity for the country than a dissolution of the Union." On January 23, 1861, he privately expressed the view that "secession is nothing but revolution."

The framers of our Constitution never exhausted so much labor, wisdom and forbearance in its formation, and surrounded it with so many guards and securities, if it was intended to be broken by every member of the confederacy at will. It was intended for "perpetual union" . . . and for the establishment of a government, not a compact, which can only be dissolved by revolution, or the consent of all the people in convention assembled. It is idle to talk of secession.

Lee did not believe there were grounds for a revolution, "I see no cause of disunion, strife and civil war," and he did not want Virginia to secede.

I am particularly anxious that Virginia should keep right, as she was chiefly instrumental in the formation and inauguration of the Constitution. So I could wish that she might be able to maintain it to save the Union.

While he was stationed in Texas, Lee watched the actions of the Southern states with dismay. He saw the Union coming apart, but he realized that he was too far away to do anything "to hasten or retard it." Lee was convinced that a civil war might last ten years, and he knew that Virginia, as a primary battleground, would be devastated. Yet, after returning home in March 1861, he never made his views known to the Virginia convention that was debating the issue of secession. While we can never know if Lee could have kept Virginia in the Union, we do know that he was highly respected. His concerns about the disastrous consequences of a civil war would certainly have been given serious consideration.

ADVICE

Some issues are so important that you need to speak out publicly.

105. CONFLICTING PRINCIPLES

*O*N APRIL 20, 1861, ONE DAY AFTER LEARNING THAT Virginia had seceded, Lee resigned from the United States Army. It had been nearly 36 years since he had begun his army career as a West Point cadet. He wrote of "the struggle it has cost me to separate myself from a service to which I have devoted all the best years of my life and all the ability I possessed." Before leaving Texas, Lee had told a Northern friend:

My loyalty to Virginia ought to take precedence over that which is due the Federal Government. . . . If Virginia stands by the old Union, so will I. But if she secedes (though I do not believe in secession as a constitutional right, nor that there is sufficient cause for revolution), then I will follow my native state with my sword, and if need be with my life. I know you think and feel very differently, but I can't help it. These are my principles, and I must follow them.

When after the war, Lee was asked if, with the benefit of hindsight, he would have acted differently, he replied, "I could have taken no other course without dishonor. And if it were all to be done over again, I should act in precisely the same manner."

A D V I C E

You may be placed in the difficult situation of having to choose among conflicting principles. You must decide in your own heart and mind, as Lee had to do in his, which principle is primary. In the final analysis, you have to do what you believe is right. Then no matter how it turns out, you need not be ashamed, and you should have no regrets.

106. "FLEXIBLE PRINCIPLES" IS AN OXYMORON

*T*WO DAYS BEFORE HE RESIGNED HIS ARMY COMMISSION, but when it had already become obvious to everyone that Virginia was going to secede, a representative of President Lincoln offered Lee command of the Union army. It was a tempting offer. Lee would command the largest army ever seen on the North American continent. He would have the rank of major general. When General Scott, who was 75, retired, Lee would become commanding general of the United States Army, and if he were victorious, there was every reason to think that he would be elected the next President of the United States. Lee didn't even need time to think it over.

I declined the offer he made me to take command of the army that was to be brought into the field, stating as candidly and as courteously as I could, that though opposed to secession and deprecating war, I could take no part in an invasion of the Southern states.

ADVICE

There are some people who have "flexible principles." That is, they'll do whatever is advantageous for them personally regardless of whether they believe it is right or wrong. Politicians of this genre will espouse whatever cause is currently popular regardless of their prior stance on the issue. They will use outright lies and half-truths to savage their opponents, and they will cut deals that are clearly not in the

best interests of their constituencies as long as they promote their political (and in some cases financial) fortunes.
There are also businessmen and women who behave this
way. It is not that they don't profess to have principles. It's
that they are willing to change their principles for personal
gain. If you have managers working for you who are similarly cavalier about their principles, get them out of your
organization as fast as you can. Chameleons don't belong in
management.

107. INSPIRE CONFIDENCE

$\mathscr{O}$N APRIL 22, 1861, LEE ACCEPTED A COMMISSION AS
major general commanding the armed forces of Virginia.
The following day he made a brief acceptance speech to
the delegates of the Virginia convention. One of them
recorded the impression Lee made:

> *Those who witnessed his appearance before the convention, saw his manly bearing, and heard the few grave, dignified and impressive words with which he consecrated himself and his sword to the cause of his native state, can never forget that scene. All felt at once that we had a leader worthy of the State and the cause.*

ADVICE

Some managers on taking a new job mistake generating
enthusiasm for inspiring confidence. They hold kickoff
meetings, give "we're going to do this, we're going to do
that, we're going to get them" speeches, and engage in all
manner of hoopla. Generating enthusiasm is good, but
when you are taking over in a tough spot, remember your
new people want reassurance first. They need to believe
you are up to the job. Getting down to work in a calm,
dignified and serious manner is the way to inspire confidence.

108. NOT WHAT'S IN IT FOR YOU

*T*HE SAME DAY LEE DELIVERED HIS ACCEPTANCE SPEECH, he met with the Confederacy's Vice President Alexander Stephens who was in Richmond negotiating Virginia's entrance into the Confederacy. Lee was a major general in Virginia, but the highest rank in the Confederacy was that of brigadier general. Stephens was concerned that Lee might raise an objection that could scuttle his negotiations. Lee told him that he believed that Virginia could not go it alone. Having seceded from the Union, it now needed to join the Confederacy. As Stephens recalled:

> *He stated, in words which produced thorough conviction in my mind of their perfect sincerity, that he did not wish anything connected with himself individually, or his official rank or personal position, to interfere in the slightest degree with the immediate consummation of that measure which he regarded as one of the utmost importance.*

ADVICE

The best leaders don't ask, "What's in it for me?" They put their organization first. John F. Kennedy's words, "ask not what your country can do for you; ask what you can do for your country," are not a platitude. They are key to the way responsible leaders conduct themselves.

109. TO GET UP AND RUNNING ASAP

*L*EE'S FIRST TASK WAS TO PREPARE VIRGINIA TO REPEL an invasion by the Union army that Lincoln was raising. A rapid mobilization was essential. He established a training camp and used cadets from the Virginia Military Institute to drill the recruits. He also established an artillery school. As officers who had resigned from the U.S. Army reported for duty, he assigned them to command the new units and continue their preparation for battle. In a matter of months, he built an army from scratch. A. L. Long gave this description of Lee's remarkable accomplishment:

Such was his wonderful talent for organization that in the space of two months he was able to equip for the field sixty regiments of infantry and cavalry, besides numerous batteries of artillery, making an aggregate of nearly 50,000 men.

ADVICE

When some companies go to open a new store or call center, they are reluctant to pull all but a few experienced managers from their on-going operations. They choose to staff the new location from the ground up. The result is that inexperienced supervisors, who didn't get the time they needed to learn their jobs, end up trying to train the new people. In the rush to become operational quickly, performance inevitably suffers. The only way to successfully get up and running as soon as possible is to put the operation in the hands of experienced supervisors and managers. That means stripping them from other parts of your organization and even paying relocation expenses, but this price is small compared to the cost of a bad start.

110. LEAVE SOME FOR LATER

*D*URING THE MOBILIZATION, LEE REFUSED TO ALLOW boys who were still in school to enlist. As he explained to his wife:

> *I could not consent to take boys from their school and young men from their colleges and put them in the ranks at the beginning of a war when they are not wanted and when there were enough men for the purpose. The war may last 10 years. Where are our ranks to be filled from then?*

A D V I C E

Manufacturers have long recognized that just because a new product or an enhancement to an existing product is ready for market doesn't mean it should be released immediately. This applies equally well in other situations. Use only what you need to now, and save the rest for the future.

111. NOT BEFORE YOU'RE READY

*E*VEN AS LEE WAS MOBILIZING VIRGINIA'S FORCES, hotheaded politicians were urging an immediate attack upon Washington or Baltimore. Lee, on the other hand, was trying not to provoke a battle before his forces were ready. He wrote to one of his commanders:

> *The policy of the State at present is strictly defensive. No attack, or provocation for attack will therefore be given, but every attack resisted to the extent of your means. . . . I must urge upon you the importance of organizing and instructing the troops as rapidly as possible and preparing them for active service.*

A D V I C E

Some companies lead with press announcements. In most instances, it is fine to announce the building of a new office, store or plant, and groundbreaking ceremonies can provide valuable free publicity. However, throwing a premature punch at the competition can be a bad mistake. Insurance agents, for example, have in the past successfully slowed the regulatory approval process for new non-agency entrants into their state who had the poor judgment to fire an advertising warning shot before their filings had been approved. Unless you have no other alternative, follow Lee's advice, "It is important that conflict be not provoked before we are ready."

112. MAKE SURE THEY KNOW HOW LONG THEY'RE IN FOR

*L*EE WANTED THE RECRUITS ENLISTED FOR AS LONG AS the war lasted. The politicians set the term of enlistment at one year. Lee clearly anticipated the problem that their short-sightedness would create. Walter H. Taylor served as one of Lee's staff officers from early May 1861 until the end of the war. He recalled:

> *He [Lee] contended that, if the conflict should terminate in twelve months, or less, the troops would be at once disbanded . . . but, if it should be prolonged beyond that period, then there would be a more urgent need for the troops . . . and the Government would have to deal with the very serious question of the disintegration and disorganization of the army, and the substitution of recruits for veterans, in the very face of the enemy.*

In the summer of 1862, with a Union army menacing Richmond, the men Lee had mustered into service the previous year, and worked so hard to train, completed their enlistment.

ADVICE

When you assemble a group for a special assignment, or when you ask people to work temporarily in a different location, make certain they understand how long you expect them to serve. Giving a person a six-month assignment is one thing. An assignment that is expected to take six months but which will require that person's presence no matter how long it takes is quite a different thing. A person who would jump at the former might find the latter intolerable, and that could cost you the services of a key performer at a critical juncture.

113. DO MORE THAN YOUR BEST

*D*URING THE MOBILIZATION, LEE HAD TO CONTEND with numerous shortages. Arms and ammunition were in short supply. During training, some recruits found themselves needing to form up, aim their muskets, and at the command to fire, shout "Bang!" Lee had to tell one man who complained about the state of his company's armament:

> *Sir, your people had better write to Mr. Lincoln and ask him to postpone this thing for a few months until you can get ready for him.*

ADVICE

From time to time, almost every organization has to deal with shortages. These are the times when you have to remind your people of Admiral Ernest J. King's instructions to the U.S. Navy after the attack on Pearl Harbor, "Do more than your best with what you've got."

114. DIFFERENT STROKES FOR DIFFERENT FOLKS

*I*N ADDITION TO MOBILIZING VIRGINIA'S FORCES, LEE was preparing plans to defend the state against attack. Foreseeing a Union march on Manassas, he ordered the officer commanding that front to

> *post at Manassas Gap Junction a force sufficient to defend that point against an attack likely to be made against it by troops from Washington. It will be necessary to give this point your personal attention.*

Brigadier General Benjamin Huger, a 36-year army veteran who had served with Lee in Mexico, was commanding the Confederate forces at Norfolk. Lee wrote to him and suggested what he should do to counter anticipated enemy troop movements:

> *The effect of either of these movements will be to cut off your communication with Richmond, and I take the liberty of calling your attention to this, as I know the pressure of the duties now upon you. I would recommend. . . .*

A D V I C E

Some managers make the mistake of treating everybody the same when it comes to giving direction. With some people you do need to give clear, explicit, direct orders. With others, only a suggestion is required. Seasoned managers, who may not have noticed some minor slippage, will probably jump right on a problem that is gently pointed out to them in the form of a reminder and recommendation. But they might resent and react negatively to a direct order that they perceive as implying incompetence on their part.

115. WHEN NOT TO BE TOO SPECIFIC

*J*OSEPH E. JOHNSTON WAS COMMANDING AT HARPERS Ferry. Johnston was concerned that he would be forced to withdraw if attacked. Lee sent him the following instructions:

It is hoped that you will be able to be timely informed of the approach of troops against you, and retire, provided they cannot be successfully opposed. You must exercise your discretion and judgment in this respect, to insure, if possible, your safety. Precise instructions cannot be given you, but, being informed of the object of the campaign, you will be able to regulate its conduct to the best advantage.

ADVICE

Some executives try to manage all their operations, including those in foreign countries, as if they were located down the hall. This is inefficient. Your managers, especially those in remote locations, need the flexibility to respond to local conditions. They know what needs to be done. Since you are not on the scene, you can't have a full appreciation of what's going on. Any detailed instructions you give are likely to miss the mark. Instead, let them exercise their discretion and judgment. On D-Day, Hitler issued several detailed orders; Eisenhower didn't issue a single one.

116. WHO GETS THE CREDIT

*L*EE ENVISIONED COORDINATED ACTION BETWEEN THE forces at Harpers Ferry and those at Manassas. His strategy proved decisive in the first major engagement of the Civil War at Manassas (Bull Run) on July 21, 1861. Lee felt "mortified" that he took no part in the battle, but he realized that the "glorious victory" the Confederate armies had won, and not his personal feelings, was what was really important.

Lee was unstinting in his praise of the victorious generals, P.G.T. Beauregard and Joseph E. Johnston, and never concerned himself that the role he had played in preparing Virginia's defenses for battle was being overlooked. Not only had Lee developed the successful strategy, he had raised, trained and equipped over 35,000 of the men who fought that day. After Lee's death, General Jubal A. Early would remark that had it not been "for the capacity and energy displayed by General Lee in organizing and equipping troops to be sent to the front, our army would not have been in a condition to gain the first victory at Manassas."

A D V I C E

It's only natural to want to receive credit for what you accomplish, but what's really important is making sure the job is done well. One of Ronald Reagan's favorite proverbs is, "A great deal of good can be done in this world if one is not too concerned about who gets the credit."

117. DO THE WORK OF THE DAY

*W*ALTER TAYLOR REMEMBERED THAT DURING THOSE trying days at the start of the war, Lee still took the time to relax. He could afford to relax at the end of each day's work because he had such an effective working style. As Taylor recalled:

> *I have never known a man more thorough and painstaking in all that he undertook. Early at his office, punctual in meeting all engagements, methodical to an extreme in his way of dispatching business, giving close attention to details, but not . . . neglectful of the more important matters . . . he seemed to address himself to the accomplishment of every task that devolved upon him in a conscientious and deliberate way, as if he himself was directly accountable to some higher power for the manner in which he performed his duty.*

> *He was not satisfied unless at the close of his office hours every matter requiring prompt attention had been disposed of.*

ADVICE

There is no substitute for a disciplined working style. The best managers are adherents to the Duke of Wellington's cardinal rule: "Do the business of the day in the day."

118. YOU CAN'T MAKE UP FOR LOST TIME

*T*OWARD THE END OF JULY 1861, JEFFERSON DAVIS SENT Lee to western Virginia. Lee received no written instructions, but as one newspaper reported, "His visit is . . . to be one of inspection, and consultation on the plan of campaign."

Lee's first stop in western Virginia was at the headquarters of General William W. Loring. He learned that Loring had a plan to drive back the Union forces. A. L. Long, who was serving on Loring's staff at the time, wrote:

> *It was obvious to all those about the general that the success of the proposed movement depended upon its speedy execution. . . . Delay would enable the Federals to seize all the important passes on the route, and fortify them so strongly that they would effectually arrest the advance of any force.*

But Loring was in no hurry to advance, and Lee was unable to convince him of the need to move quickly. As a result, the best opportunity the Confederates had in western Virginia was lost. Lee told his wife:

> *It is so difficult to get our people, unaccustomed to the necessities of war, to comprehend and promptly execute the measures required for the occasion.*

A D V I C E

Lost time is an unrecoverable resource. Good managers look for ways to gain time, while bad managers fritter it away.

While he was in western Virginia, Lee grew his famous beard. The following summer, he described his appearance in a letter to his daughter-in-law: "My coat is of gray, of the regulation style and pattern. . . . I have the same handsome hat which surmounts my gray head (the latter is not prescribed in the regulations) and shields my ugly face, which is masked by a white beard as stiff and wiry as the teeth of a [cotton] card. In fact an uglier person you have never seen, and so unattractive is it to our enemies that they shoot at it whenever visible to them."

ORING HAD SERVED WITH DISTINCTION IN THE
Mexican War. He went on to command a regiment and the
Department of New Mexico. A. L. Long believed that the
reason Loring refused to follow Lee's advice was because
he felt bitter that Lee outranked him. According to Long,
"Having been his [Lee's] superior in rank in the old army,
he could not suppress a feeling of jealousy."

Lee believed in giving someone a second chance, especially if the mistake the person had made was due to inexperience or extenuating circumstances. While at Loring's
headquarters, he was asked what to do about a soldier who
had fallen asleep while on guard duty. Lee told the officer:

You know the arduous duties these men have to do daily.
Suppose the man who was found on his post asleep had been
you, or me. What do you think should be done to him?

However, Lee viewed Loring's behavior as quite another
matter. In October 1862, when Lee was commanding the
Army of Northern Virginia, he informed the Secretary of War:

I have no position in this army for General Loring.

A D V I C E

To err is human, but errors that result from certain kinds of
behavior do not deserve to be forgiven.

In May 1861, when Virginia joined the Confederacy, Lee had been appointed
a brigadier general and shortly thereafter a full general. That appointment was
confirmed on August 31st. At which time, by the date of his commission, Lee
became the Confederate Army's third highest ranking officer, after Samuel
Cooper and Albert Sidney Johnston.

120. QUESTIONABLE SOURCES

*I*N EARLY SEPTEMBER 1861, LEE LEARNED FROM Colonel Albert Rust of a path that led to a position from which an attack could be successfully made on the Union forces on Cheat Mountain. Rust asked for the honor of leading the attack. Once the firing began on Cheat Mountain, the other units would advance.

Rust got his men into position on the night of September 11th and prepared to attack the following morning. That evening his men captured several Union pickets who informed Rust that the Union commander knew he was going to attack, that there were 4000–5000 Union troops in strong defensive positions waiting for him, and that reinforcements were on the way. Rust would later report that since "the enemy had four times my force" it would have been "madness to make an attack." Because Rust decided not to attack, the rest of Lee's plan had to be abandoned. In reality there were about 300 Union soldiers on Cheat Mountain.

A D V I C E

Never accept at face value information that comes from questionable sources.

Lee had not known Rust previously. You should never entrust a critically important assignment to someone whose experience and judgment are question marks in your book.

121. WE HAVE MET THE ENEMY, AND HE IS US

*L*EE HAD HIS HANDS FULL IN WESTERN VIRGINIA WITH two feuding politicians who had been made instant generals. They seemed more interested in fighting with each other than with the real enemy. Of these two political generals, John B. Floyd and Henry A. Wise, one man commented, "I am fully satisfied that each of them would be highly gratified to see the other annihilated. It would be just as easy to combine oil and water as to expect a union of action between these gentlemen."

General Floyd was the senior officer, but General Wise refused to obey his orders. Wise insisted on acting as if his forces constituted an independent command. Lee tried to reason with Wise. On August 8, 1861, Lee told him:

In regard to your request to separate the commands of General Floyd and yourself . . . it would . . . destroy the prospect of the success of the campaign . . . . Our enemy is so strong at all points that we can only hope to give him an effective blow by a concentration of our forces. . . . I hope . . . you will join General Floyd, and take that part in the campaign which may be assigned your brigade.

On September 21st, he was still trying to get Wise to obey orders:

Our united forces are not more than one half of the strength of the enemy. Together they may not be able to withstand his assault. . . . I beg therefore that the troops be united.

On September 25th, Jefferson Davis resolved the issue by relieving Wise of command and ordering him to report to Richmond.

ADVICE

The only way to deal with insubordinate managers is to relieve them of their responsibilities. Depending on the underlying cause of the insubordination, it may be possible to reassign them to other duties.

122. MANAGEMENT, NOT COORDINATION

$\mathcal{L}$EE RETURNED TO RICHMOND AT THE END OF OCTOBER. While he had succeeded in preventing the enemy from advancing, he had been unsuccessful in driving them back. On October 24, 1861, the people of western Virginia voted to secede from Virginia and join the Union as the State of West Virginia. Lee's first field assignment for the Confederacy had ended in failure.

The situation that confronted Lee when he had arrived in western Virginia was dismal. The terrain was mountainous, the roads were nearly impassable due to heavy rains, and the population overwhelmingly supported the Union. The three small Confederate armies in the region were ill equipped, short of supplies, and their ranks were decimated by disease.

Lee must have realized that unless a competent senior officer was placed in overall command of the Confederate forces, there was no hope of driving the Union army out of western Virginia. He has been criticized for not assuming command himself, but his instructions precluded his taking command. Lee had been given a temporary assignment as a coordinator. Only a month after arriving at the front, Lee received a message from Adjutant and Inspector General Samuel Cooper telling him that President Davis "has not ceased to feel an anxious desire for your return to this city to resume your former duties."

Rather than asking Lee to coordinate the operations in western Virginia, Jefferson Davis should have put him in command. Years later, Davis wrote that he had hoped that Lee's "deserved influence over men" would have enabled him to be successful in western Virginia. It was a forlorn hope.

A D V I C E

Important projects need to be managed, not coordinated.

Lee was reluctant to speak candidly about what had happened in western Virginia. Davis wrote that Lee "was unwilling to offend anyone who was wearing a sword and striking blows for the Confederacy." When you ask your senior people to review other managers' operations, make sure they clearly understand that it is essential for you to receive a candid, confidential assessment of any problems they uncover. You can't manage an organization effectively if your people are reluctant to surface problems for fear of offending someone.

123. WHAT HAVE YOU DONE FOR ME LATELY?

*W*HEN LEE BECAME COMMANDER OF VIRGINIA'S ARMED forces in April 1861, the State's newspapers were ecstatic. The following editorial appeared in the *Alexandria Gazette* and the *Richmond Dispatch*. It is typical of the praise that was heaped upon him:

> *an able, brave, experienced officer—no man his superior in all that constitutes the soldier and the gentleman—no man more worthy to head our forces and lead our army. There is no man who would command more of the confidence of the people of Virginia, than this distinguished officer; and no one under whom the volunteers and militia would more gladly rally. His reputation, his acknowledged ability, his chivalric character, his probity, honor, and—may we add, to his eternal praise—his Christian life and conduct—make his name a "tower of strength."*

In June, commenting on Lee's efforts to mobilize Virginia's forces, an editor for the *Richmond Dispatch* wrote:

> *When General Lee assumed the command of affairs here everyone knows that our military preparations were in a condition which it makes us shudder to look back upon. . . . We may point with honest pride to the position Virginia is now in for defense and claim that even General Scott . . . has not proved himself as great and efficient a leader as . . . the sagacious, intrepid and high-souled chieftain of Virginia.*

By September, unhappy with his apparent inaction in western Virginia, the editorials were referring to him as "Granny Lee." A mid-October editorial in the *Charleston*

Mercury opined, "The people are getting mighty sick of this dilly-dally . . . so much so that they will demand that . . . [Lee] be brought back and permitted to pay court to the ladies." After the campaign ended, one journalist summarized it in these words:

The most remarkable circumstance of this campaign was that it was conducted by a general who had never fought a battle, who had a pious horror of guerillas, and whose extreme tenderness of blood induced him to depend exclusively upon the resources of strategy.

Lee did not respond publicly, but he did tell his wife, "I am sorry . . . the movements of the armies cannot keep pace with the expectations of the editors of papers."

A D V I C E

While it is most apparent in sports and politics, the press, and consequently the public, have a short memory. Some business reporters will focus on a company's most recent quarterly earnings or current labor problems and ignore its long-term track record. Being beaten up by the press shouldn't get you down, and being the darling of the press shouldn't puff you up. During a football game, shortly after the press dubbed Notre Dame's backfield "the four horsemen," Knute Rockne had his first string line sit on the bench. When his backfield stars complained that they were getting killed by the opposing linemen, Rockne suggested they show the other team their newspaper clippings.

Managers can also suffer from short memory syndrome. Systems staffs are often berated for a single outage even when the systems they maintain have been performing without a hitch for many months. Just because the press has a "what have you done for me lately" mentality doesn't mean you should.

159

124. DOES IT SELL NEWSPAPERS?

*L*EE WAS TROUBLED BY THE LEAKS AND INACCURACIES that appeared in the press. Strategic and tactical plans, troop movements and troop strength were regularly reported in the papers even though such information was of enormous value to the enemy. In October 1861, Lee lost the opportunity for a surprise attack on the Union army because his detailed plan of attack was printed in a Richmond newspaper. In a letter to his son, Custis, describing conditions in western Virginia, Lee wrote, "Do not mention this. I pray you. It will be in the papers next."

He told his wife to regard all press reports with care:

You will see there more than ever occurs, and what does [appear in the newspapers] must be taken with much allowance.

A D V I C E

The year the Civil War began, the *Chicago Times* expressed the view that it was a "newspaper's duty to . . . raise hell." You need to assume that any information given to the media, or to someone who might accidentally or intentionally leak it to the media, is going to be reported. This includes data provided on an off-the-record basis. The less said to the press the better, not only to protect proprietary information, but also because anything you say is subject to being twisted and distorted for the sake of making the story fit a predisposed bias, or simply to make it more interesting.

125. ARMCHAIR EXPERTS

*R*EGARDING THE PROPENSITY OF NEWSPAPER EDITORS
to always know what should have been done, Lee told a
friend:

> *We made a great mistake. . . . We appointed all our*
> *worst generals to command the armies, and all our best*
> *generals to edit the newspapers. As you know, I have*
> *planned some campaigns and quite a number of battles. I*
> *have given the work all the care and thought I could, and*
> *sometimes, when my plans were completed, they seemed to*
> *be perfect. But when I have fought them through, I have*
> *discovered defects and occasionally wondered I did not see*
> *some of the defects in advance. When it was all over, I*
> *found by reading a newspaper that these best editor gener-*
> *als saw all the defects plainly from the start. Unfortunately,*
> *they did not communicate their knowledge to me until it*
> *was too late. . . . I have done the best I could in the field,*
> *and have not succeeded as I could wish. I am willing to*
> *yield my place to these best generals, and I will do my best*
> *for the cause editing a newspaper.*

A D V I C E

Analyze what happened. Decide what might have been
done differently, and what you would do if faced with a
similar situation. But don't be an armchair quarterback and
presume that you could have done better. Even if you think
you could have, keep it to yourself.

126. GIVE THEM A FRESH START

*I*N NOVEMBER 1861, LEE WAS GIVEN COMMAND OF THE Confederacy's southeastern coastal defenses. His reputation had been severely damaged by the press reports of his activities in western Virginia. Jefferson Davis was concerned about the effect that this would have on Lee's ability to carry out his new assignment. As Davis recalled:

> *Lest the newspaper attack should have created unjust and unfavorable impressions in regard to him, I thought it desirable to write to Governor [Francis W.] Pickens and tell him what manner of man he was who had been sent to South Carolina.*

ADVICE

When you give a new assignment to someone who is coming off a job that went poorly, let everyone know that he or she still enjoys your full confidence and support.

127. FIRST THE BAD NEWS, THEN . . .

*S*HORTLY AFTER ARRIVING IN SOUTH CAROLINA, LEE reported that the Union fleet had entered Port Royal Harbor. The troops defending Hilton Head had been withdrawn, but "their tents, clothing, and provisions, were mostly lost, and all the guns."

The enemy having complete possession of the water and inland navigation, commands all the islands on this coast, and threatens both Savannah and Charleston. . . . We have no guns that can resist their batteries . . . .

In his report Lee included the steps he was taking to deal with this emergency.

I am endeavoring to bring into the field . . . .

ADVICE

Always report the bad news promptly and completely. At the same time let your boss know what you intend to do about it.

128. SPREAD TOO THIN

*L*EE REALIZED THAT UNDER THE HEAVY GUNS OF THE
Union fleet, the enemy could strike with impunity any-
where along the coast. He therefore decided to abandon
"all exposed points as far as possible within range of the
enemy's fleet" and take defensive positions further inland
where he could engage the Union army "on more equal
terms." As he reported:

> *The guns from the less important points have been
> removed, and are employed in strengthening those consid-
> ered of greater consequence. . . . At all these places there is
> much yet to be done, but every effort is being made to ren-
> der them as strong as the nature of the position and the
> means at hand will permit. They ought after their comple-
> tion to make a good defense against any batteries that are
> likely to be brought against them.*

A D V I C E

You can't be all things to all people. There is a limit to how
many products you can produce, or how many markets you
can be in. Concentrate on your core competencies and the
distribution channels or geographic areas that enable you to
make the greatest inroads.

129. IT'S NOT A POPULARITY CONTEST

*A*s CONFEDERATE UNITS WERE MUSTERED INTO SERVICE, it was common for the men to elect their officers. Lee was opposed to this practice.

The best troops are ineffective without good officers. Our volunteers . . . require officers whom they can respect and trust . . . . It would be safe to trust men of the intelligence and character of our volunteers to elect their officers, could they at the time of election realize their dependent condition in the day of battle. But this they cannot do, and I have known them in the hour of danger repudiate and disown officers of their choice and beg for others. Is it right, then, for a State to throw upon its citizens a responsibility which they . . . cannot properly exercise? . . . I think it better for the field officers of the regiments . . . to be appointed.

ADVICE

The persons you promote should have the respect of their peers, but they don't have to be (probably shouldn't be) the most popular kids on the block. Gladhanders rarely possess the ability to say "no" that all good leaders must have.

130. NO ONE IS GOING TO SAVE YOU

*W*HEN LEE'S WIFE EXPRESSED THE HOPE THAT
Great Britain and the Union would go to war, Lee told her:

> *You must not build your hopes on peace on account of*
> *the United States going into a war with England. She will*
> *be very loath to do that, notwithstanding the bluster of the*
> *Northern papers . . . . We must make up our minds to fight*
> *our battles and win our independence alone. No one will*
> *help us.*

ADVICE

Some executives delude themselves into thinking that all
their problems would go away if only they could find the
right acquisition, joint venture, merger or strategic partner.
Such measures can temporarily obscure a company's fundamental weaknesses, but unless those weaknesses are
addressed, the benefit is a short-lived public relations one
at best. Clean up your own mess. Don't look for someone
else to save you.

131. WHEN THE GOING GETS TOUGH

*W*HEN HE LEARNED THAT UNION FORCES IN TENNESSEE had captured Fort Donelson, Lee wrote:

> *The news . . . is not all cheering, and disasters seem to be thickening around us. It calls for renewed energies and redoubled strength on our part.*

ADVICE

The leader sets the tone for the rest of the organization. When things are going badly, you can't allow yourself to become depressed and listless. You need to pull yourself together and redouble your efforts.

To one of his sons, Lee had written, "Shake off those gloomy feelings. Drive them away. . . . Look upon things as they are. Take them as you find them. Make the best of them. Turn them to your advantage."

132. GROUSING

$\mathcal{T}$HE GENERAL IN CHARGE OF THE DEFENSES AT
Charleston, Roswell S. Ripley, really disliked Lee. His out-
spoken anti-Lee sentiments prompted Governor Pickens to
write President Davis:

> *I take the liberty to inform you that I fear the feeling
> of General Ripley towards General Lee may do injury to
> the public service. His habit is to say extreme things even
> before junior officers, and this is well calculated to do great
> injury to General Lee's command.*

ADVICE

It is unbecoming for a manager to grouse about his or her
boss. Think about the message you send to the people
reporting to you when you criticize the person you're working for.

133. PARADIGM SHIFTING TECHNOLOGY

*L*EE'S FIRST ASSIGNMENT AFTER GRADUATING FROM West Point had been to assist in the construction of a fort for the defense of Savannah. When it was finally completed in 1847, Fort Pulaski, built with 25 million bricks, was considered impregnable. Nonetheless, Lee prepared additional fortifications nearer to Savannah.

In early March 1862, Lee received orders to report to Richmond for a new assignment. One month later, Union artillery, using ordnance that had been developed in the fifteen years since the completion of Fort Pulaski, pounded the fort into rubble.

ADVICE

Brick and mortar companies can find themselves caught flatfooted by new technologies that enable new entrants to shift the paradigms of their businesses. Companies that are reluctant to invest in overhauling their huge legacy systems are particularly vulnerable since they are unlikely to be able to take advantage of the new technologies.

1

TO BOLDLY
GO . . .

March–July 1862

In March 1862, Lee becomes the military advisor to President Jefferson Davis. He oversees the rapid redeployment of Confederate troops to meet a Union advance on Richmond. He also devises the strategy that successfully prevents the Union army in northern Virginia from moving south and linking up with the forces threatening Richmond.

When General Joseph E. Johnston is wounded, Lee takes over command of the Army of Northern Virginia, and develops and executes a daring plan that defeats General George B. McClellan's larger and better equipped Union army. Although acclaimed for his victory in the Seven Days campaign, Lee is disappointed that the Union army was not destroyed.

*I*N MARCH 1862, LEE RETURNED TO RICHMOND IN HIS
new role as military advisor to President Davis. Ever since
the initial victory at the first battle of Manassas, the
Confederacy had suffered one military defeat after another.
Now Union General George B. McClellan was preparing to
invade Virginia with the largest army that had ever been
assembled on the North American continent. Not only
were the Confederates outnumbered, but also the men who
had joined the army at the beginning of the war were completing their terms of enlistment, and many were planning
to go home rather than reenlist.

A number of military and political leaders believed that
the ranks would be filled if adequate incentives, in the form
of bonuses and furloughs, were provided to encourage reen-
listment. Lee knew that the time for volunteerism had passed.
He had one of his aides, Charles Marshall, draw up a bill
requiring all white males between the ages of 18 and 45 to
serve in the armed forces for the duration of the war. The
Confederate Congress enacted a watered-down version of the
bill that provided numerous exemptions from military service.

A D V I C E

When desperate measures are called for, you cannot take
half steps. In some ways they are worse than doing nothing
because they lull you into a false sense of security.

One measure that Lee favored was the enlistment of blacks, but the Confederate
Congress refused to let them serve in the army until it was too late. Some members
of Congress didn't want slaves in the army because they believed that blacks were
inferior to whites. For others the problem was that you couldn't expect slaves to
fight for the Confederacy unless you were willing to give them their freedom. This
posed no problem for Lee who told a friend, "If the slaves of the South were mine,
I would surrender them all without a struggle to avert this war."

135. RAPID DEPLOYMENT

*L*EE EXPECTED GENERAL MCCLELLAN TO LAND HIS army in southeastern Virginia and either attempt to capture Norfolk or move up the Peninsula and lay siege to Richmond. Since the forces on the Peninsula were too weak to oppose such a movement, Lee needed to rapidly redeploy the Confederate forces in Virginia and the Carolinas to meet this threat.

Our army is in the fermentation of reorganization. I . . . am endeavoring by every means in my power to bring our troops and hasten them to their destination.

To secure the prompt cooperation of the commanders whose troops were being redeployed, Lee took pains to explain the rationale for his orders.

General: I regret very much to be obliged to reduce the force in your department. . . . But from present appearances it will be necessary to collect additional troops to oppose the advance of the enemy, who has now reached the Rappahannock [River], and may move upon Richmond from that direction as well as from the coast, where he is assembling large bodies of troops.

A D V I C E

Business executives need to be concerned about their organization's ability to adapt rapidly to changing or unforeseen circumstances. These can range from a catastrophe that closes an office, or requires sending extra teams into the field, to shifting call center or store personnel to deal with unanticipated demand. You need to have good contingency plans, but they will be ineffective unless your people understand the need and the importance of responding quickly.

136. KILL TWO BIRDS WITH ONE STONE

*W*HEN ONE GENERAL IN NORTH CAROLINA OBJECTED TO sending a part of his force to Virginia, Lee explained:

> *The need for troops in the vicinity of Fredericksburg is very urgent, and they can contribute to the defense of North Carolina as materially at that point, as they would in assisting to prevent an advance from the enemy now occupying the eastern waters of [North Carolina].*

ADVICE

You can sometimes achieve two goals simultaneously, one directly, and the other as a byproduct of doing the first.

137. USE A WIDE-ANGLE LENS

*E*VEN THOUGH THE SITUATION IN VIRGINIA WAS CRITICAL, Lee kept his eye on the other theaters of operation. To General John C. Pemberton, who was commanding in South Carolina, Georgia and Florida, he telegraphed:

> *[General P. G. T.] Beauregard is pressed for troops. Send, if possible, [General Daniel S.] Donelson's brigade . . . to Corinth. If Mississippi Valley is lost Atlantic states will be ruined.*

ADVICE

No matter how pressing any one area of concern is, you must not lose sight of the operations in other areas.

138. BLUFF

*G*ENERAL JOHN B. MAGRUDER WAS COMMANDING THE Confederate forces on the Peninsula. He was vastly out-numbered, but until Lee could reinforce him, he needed to hold his position. Lee suggested that he bluff.

General: Notwithstanding the demonstrations of the enemy in your front, I see nothing to prove that he intends immediately to attempt your line. He is feeling your strength. . . . I hope you will so maneuver as to deceive and thwart him.

Magruder marched his men in and out of the view of the Union army giving the impression that large numbers of fresh troops were arriving daily. He created earthworks bristling with logs that at a distance appeared to be cannon. The ever-cautious General McClellan, rather than immedi-ately attacking, waited for his heavy guns to be brought up. This gave Lee the precious time he needed to complete the movement of troops to the Peninsula.

A D V I C E

Bluffing is a legitimate tactic. Your understanding of the other party must be good enough to let you accurately assess your chances of being successful. Since there is the possibility that your bluff will be called, you should always leave yourself a back door.

*I*N ADDITION TO MCCLELLAN'S ARMY ON THE PENINSULA, the Confederates were also threatened from the north by the Union army commanded by General Irwin McDowell. If McDowell moved south and linked up with McClellan, the Union forces advancing on Richmond would outnumber the Confederate defenders by two to one. To prevent this from happening, Lee told General Thomas J. (Stonewall) Jackson to attack the Union army under the command of General Nathaniel P. Banks in the Shenandoah Valley. If he defeated Banks, Jackson was to advance in the direction of Washington, D.C., so as to create the illusion that he planned to attack the Capital.

Whatever movements you make against Banks do it speedily, and if successful, drive him back towards the Potomac, and create the impression as far as practicable that you design threatening that line.

Jackson's Valley campaign was so successful that the U.S. Secretary of War, Edwin M. Stanton, not only halted McDowell from moving to join McClellan, he ordered nearly half of McDowell's army to the Shenandoah Valley, and he called for troops to be rushed to the defense of Washington. To the Governor of Massachusetts, he wrote:

Intelligence from various quarters leaves no doubt that the enemy in great force are marching on Washington. You will please organize and forward immediately all the militia and volunteer forces in your State.

McDowell and McClellan realized that Washington was in no danger, and that by withdrawing McDowell's force from the advance on Richmond, President Lincoln and Secretary Stanton were passing up an opportunity for almost certain victory and an early end to the war. In response to the order to withdraw, McDowell wrote, "This is a crushing blow to us."

A D V I C E

It's good to divert your competitors. If, as a result, they panic and move precipitously to meet a nonexistent threat, so much the better. For example, nothing prevents you from publicly investigating a market or locale that you currently have no intention of entering, while privately advancing your plans to enter another.

140. ON LOCATING THE OFFICE

$\mathcal{T}$HE FIRST CAPITAL OF THE CONFEDERATE STATES OF America had been Montgomery, Alabama, a relatively safe location in the deep South. After Virginia joined the Confederacy, the capital was moved to Richmond, an exposed location, practically on the front lines. The defense of Richmond thus became of paramount importance. According to Walter Taylor, Lee realized

> *the inevitable doom that sooner or later awaited the Confederates in their inflexible purpose to hold the city of Richmond. General Lee was opposed to that policy which designated certain points as indispensable to be held, except so far and so long as they possessed strategic value to the armies operating in the field. He maintained that the determination to retain possession of such under all circumstances and at any cost caused a fallacious value to attach to success, and, in the event of failure, entailed a moral loss on us and assured an elation to the enemy altogether disproportionate to the material benefit to be derived from continued possession.*

ADVICE

Selecting an office location is an important matter. The site should be selected for sound business reasons, such as the availability of skilled workers. It shouldn't be determined by where the general manager lives, plans to retire, enjoys skiing, or can play golf all year long.

141. NO PAIN, NO GAIN

ENERAL JOSEPH E. JOHNSTON WAS RETREATING BEFORE General McClellan, who was slowly advancing toward Richmond. President Davis kept urging Johnston to attack, but Johnston, believing that the risk of failure was too great, was waiting for a better opportunity. Some Southerners were concerned that Johnston wouldn't fight unless conditions were perfect. One man who had been on a hunting trip with him recalled that although Johnston was an excellent shot,

> *the bird flew too high or low, the dogs were too far or too near. Things never did suit exactly. He was too fussy, too hard to please, too cautious, too much afraid to miss and risk his fine reputation for a crack shot. . . . Unless his ways are changed, he'll never fight a battle.*

ADVICE

You want conditions that favor success, but if you insist on conditions that guarantee success, you'll never proceed with any new venture. You may be able to avoid stubbing your toe by standing still, but you won't make any progress.

142. DO YOUR JOB FIRST

*O*N MAY 30, 1862, WITH THE UNION ARMY LESS THAN TEN miles from Richmond and a major battle in the offing, Lee had A. L. Long deliver a message to Johnston. As Long recalled, he told Johnston that Lee

> *would be glad to participate in the battle. He had no desire to interfere with his command, but simply wished to aid him on the field to the best of his ability and in any manner in which his services would be of most value. General Johnston expressed . . . the hope that General Lee would . . . send him all the reinforcements he could.*

ADVICE

It's natural to want to get in on the action, and if your duties allow you to offer assistance to another manager, then do so. But make certain that lending someone else a hand won't interfere with your primary responsibilities.

143. WHEN YOU CAN'T STAND YOUR BOSS

*S*INCE JOHNSTON'S VICTORY AT THE FIRST BATTLE OF Manassas, relations between him and President Davis had steadily deteriorated. Both men had large, easily bruised egos. Johnston felt that Davis had treated him unfairly with respect to his seniority among the five full generals of the Confederacy. Davis was irritated because he believed that Johnston was insubordinate and kept him in the dark regarding his plans.

On May 31st, Johnston attacked McClellan at Seven Pines (Fair Oaks). Lee was at Johnston's headquarters when President Davis rode up. One officer recalled what happened next:

General Johnston saw Mr. Davis approaching, and . . . sought to avoid a meeting by mounting quickly and riding rapidly to the extreme front.

While at the front, Johnston was seriously wounded.

ADVICE

When you can't stand the sight of your boss, it's time to get another job.

144. DON'T OPEN THE FIRST ENVELOPE

*W*ITH RICHMOND THREATENED AND GENERAL JOHNSTON wounded, Jefferson Davis finally gave Lee his chance to command an army. On June 1, 1862, Lee issued his first order to the Army of Northern Virginia:

> *The unfortunate casualty that has deprived the army in front of Richmond of the valuable services of its able general is not more deeply deplored by any member of his command than by its present commander. He hopes his absence will be but temporary.*

ADVICE

You may be familiar with the three-envelope story in which a manager, upon taking a difficult assignment, is given three sealed envelopes with instructions to open one of them whenever faced with a dire situation. When circumstances force the manager into opening the first envelope, the contents read, "Blame your predecessor."

Never open the first envelope. Those who didn't like their former boss won't think any more of you for attacking him or her, and you will get off on the wrong foot with those who did like your predecessor. Trying to assign blame for the problems you've inherited serves no purpose. The job is yours now. Begin by looking forward, not back.

The contents of the second and third envelopes read, "Blame the system" and "Prepare three envelopes."

145. EARN THEIR RESPECT

*L*EE'S APPOINTMENT TO COMMAND THE ARMY OF Northern Virginia was not greeted with enthusiasm. One Richmond paper commented, "Evacuating Lee, who has never yet risked a single battle with the invader, is commanding general." In his initial order to the army, Lee had stated that while he would "endeavor to the best of his ability to perform his duties" he could only be successful if he received "the cordial support of every officer and man." Realizing that the support he would require couldn't be ordered, Lee set out to earn it. As General James Longstreet recalled:

> *Lee was seen almost daily riding over his lines, making suggestions to working parties and encouraging their efforts. . . . Above all, they soon began to look eagerly for his daily rides, his pleasing yet commanding presence, and the energy he displayed in speeding their labors.*

ADVICE

You can order people to obey you, but to be successful you need more than obedience. You need the respect that engenders wholehearted support, and you can't demand that; you have to earn it. When taking over a new organization, get out on the floor, walk through the work areas, and get to meet the staff. Making the effort to be accessible and visible is an important first step to earning your people's respect.

146. MAKE THEM FEEL INVOLVED

THE DAY AFTER TAKING COMMAND, LEE HELD A meeting with his division and brigade commanders. General Longstreet was concerned that having a meeting with such a large group (about 40 officers) was dangerous because "public discussion and secrecy were incompatible." Lee, however, wasn't using the meeting to discuss his plans. He listened quietly as each officer expressed his views on the military situation and reported the status of his command.

When one officer recommended that the army retreat because it was within range of the enemy's artillery, Lee responded:

If we leave this line because they can shell us, we shall leave the next for the same reason, and I don't see how we can stop this side of Richmond.

ADVICE

When taking a new assignment, make your people feel that you are interested in their views and intend to involve them in the planning process. Your initial impressions of your new staff will be based on their understanding of the current situation, and the recommendations they make at their initial meetings with you. Careful questioning and even more careful listening will reveal much about the capabilities and temperaments of each of them.

147. COMPETITOR ASSESSMENTS

ENERAL McCLELLAN VIEWED THE APPOINTMENT OF Lee to replace Johnston as a positive development. He had served under Lee in Mexico and believed he knew him. McClellan wrote to President Lincoln that Lee was

> *too cautious and weak under grave responsibility—personally brave and energetic to a fault, he yet is wanting in moral firmness when pressed by heavy responsibility and is likely to be timid and irresolute in action.*

ADVICE

Accurate competitor assessments are critical if you are to succeed. Be careful not to rely on outdated knowledge. A person's behavior can change over time or under different circumstances. Assess your current competitor, not the shadow of his or her past self.

148. TO BOLDLY GO . . .

E. P. Edward Porter Alexander, an artillery officer with the Army of Northern Virginia, remembered asking Joseph C. Ives, an officer on Jefferson Davis' staff, Joseph C. Ives, the following question:

Ives, tell me this. We are here fortifying our lines, but apparently leaving the enemy all the time he needs to accumulate his superior forces, and then to move on us in the way he thinks best. Has General Lee the audacity that is going to be required for our inferior force to meet the enemy's superior force—to take the aggressive, and to run risks and stand chances?

Ives replied:

Alexander, if there is one man in either army . . . head and shoulders above every other in audacity it is General Lee! His name might be Audacity. He will take more desperate chances and take them quicker than any other general in this country, North or South, and you will live to see it, too.

Five days after taking command, Lee wrote to President Davis:

It will require 100,000 men to resist the regular siege of Richmond, which perhaps would only prolong not save it. I am preparing a line that I can hold with part of our forces in front, while with the rest I will endeavor to make a diversion to bring McClellan out.

What Lee was proposing was to bring Stonewall Jackson's army from the Shenandoah Valley to join with his in attacking the right flank of McClellan's army. This meant that the Valley, northern Virginia and Richmond would be left virtually defenseless. McClellan's army of 105,000 men was not only better armed and equipped than Lee's, it outnumbered his by a margin of five to four.

Davis was concerned that McClellan, finding the bulk of the Confederate army on his right flank, might move directly on Richmond, which would be too weakly defended to resist his attack. As Davis recalled, Lee responded that if the city's defenders held on for as long as they could, he would "be upon the enemy's heels" before they got to Richmond.

A D V I C E

You need to be bold without being rash or reckless. Timid souls rarely can point to a solid record of accomplishment.

Confederate and Union army strength and casualty figures throughout are approximate.

149. START WHEN THEY'RE FRESH

*T*O DRIVE THE INVADERS AWAY FROM RICHMOND
would require hard fighting. In his first order, Lee had
made it clear that he wanted his army put in the best possible shape prior to the start of the campaign.

> *Commanders of divisions and brigades will take every*
> *precaution and use every means in their power to have their*
> *commands in readiness at all times for immediate action.*
> *They will be careful to preserve their men as much as possi-*
> *ble, that they may be fresh when called upon for active serv-*
> *ice. All surplus baggage, broken down wagons . . . and*
> *everything that may embarrass the prompt and speedy*
> *movement of the army will be turned into depot.*

ADVICE

The success of a project hinges on careful, detailed and
complete preparation. It's foolish to start an important project with tired people and worn-out equipment.

150. ENCOURAGEMENT, NOT ORDERS

ONE OF LEE'S AIDES SUGGESTED THAT THE WORK OF building the fortifications around Richmond would be completed more quickly if he resorted to stern disciplinary measures rather than simply encouraging the men. Lee replied:

There is a great difference between mercenary armies and volunteer armies, and consequently there must be a difference in the mode of discipline. The volunteer army is more easily disciplined by encouraging a patriotic spirit than by a strict enforcement of the Articles of War.

ADVICE

Most people want to do a good job. In the right work environment, they only need direction, guidance and encouragement to give you their best efforts.

151. GATHER INTELLIGENCE

*L*EE PLANNED TO ATTACK THE UNION ARMY'S RIGHT
flank, but he needed to be certain of the exact position of
McClellan's forces and of the nature of the terrain that his
men would be crossing and fighting on. Lee sent Jeb Stuart
on a mission "to gain intelligence for the guidance of future
operations."

*You are desired to make a secret movement to the rear
of the enemy . . . with a view of gaining intelligence of his
operations, communications, etc. . . . You will return as soon
as the object of your expedition is accomplished and you
must . . . be content to accomplish all the good you can,
without feeling it necessary to obtain all that might be
desired.*

A D V I C E

Intelligence must be accurate, but it also must be timely,
and there is a fine balance that has to be struck between
the two. If you keep waiting until you have perfect intelligence, you will be paralyzed into inaction. You want credible data on which to base your decisions, but then you need
to proceed with the understanding that you will have to
modify your detailed plans as new information comes to
light.

152. KNOW WHAT YOUR COMPETITOR KNOWS

*B*EFORE LEE COULD ATTACK MCCLELLAN, HE NEEDED to bring Stonewall Jackson's army from the Shenandoah Valley to Richmond. There was the possibility that McClellan might attack before Jackson arrived. Lee was not worried. He told an aide:

We hear from the Federal newspapers and our spies that McClellan is prevented from advancing by the softness of the ground and his belief that he has a greatly superior force in his front.

ADVICE

In business, it is unethical to place spies in a competitor's organization. But it is perfectly acceptable to read your competitors' publications, and attend trade shows and conferences to hear what the loose tongues are saying. People often gossip, and managers who might zealously guard their companies' secrets are often only too willing to share what they know about another competitor.

153. ON BEING TOO SECRETIVE

*L*EE'S PLAN HINGED ON BRINGING JACKSON'S ARMY from the Shenandoah Valley to Richmond. He wrote to Jackson:

> *To be efficacious the movement must be secret. Let me know the force you can bring and be careful to guard from friends and foes your purpose. . . . The country is full of spies and our plans are immediately carried to the enemy.*

Jackson liked to say, "If my coat knew my plans . . . I would take it off and burn it. And if I can deceive my friends, I can make certain of deceiving my enemies." He was so secretive by nature that he didn't even share his plans to leave the Shenandoah Valley with his immediate subordinates. This caused one of his generals, Richard S. Ewell, to complain, "Jackson is driving us mad. He don't say a word . . . no hint of where we're going."

When Lee assigned General A. (Ambrose) P. Hill to Jackson in July 1862, he took the opportunity to caution Jackson not to carry his penchant for secrecy too far.

> *A. P. Hill you will find, I think, a good officer with whom you can consult and by advising with your division commanders as to your movements much trouble will be saved you in arranging details as they can act more intelligently.*

ADVICE

It is always a mistake to assume that just because someone can be trusted with sensitive information, they should be allowed access to it. The cardinal rule when dealing with confidential data is to share it only with those who have an absolute need to know. However, secrecy can be carried too far. If you wait until the last minute to share your plans with the people who will have to carry them out, you deprive yourself of their input, you make it harder for them to act intelligently, and you run the risk of lessening their effectiveness.

154. MIDDLE OF THE NIGHT COURAGE

*L*EE PLANNED TO ATTACK ON JUNE 26, 1862. ON THE 25th, Union troops probed Lee's defenses. This gave Lee cause for concern. As he explained to President Davis:

I fear from the operations of the enemy yesterday that our plan of operations has been discovered to them. It seemed to be his purpose, by his advance on our right yesterday, to discover whether our force on that front had been diminished.

Lee had moved the bulk of his forces to attack McClellan's right flank. In so doing, he had exposed his right, which was now very weakly defended. Although anxious, Lee "determined to make no change in the plan." He ordered the general commanding the portion of the front that had been probed "to hold his lines at all hazards, and to . . . [make] every preparation to meet any attack of the enemy in the morning."

ADVICE

Good leaders have "three o'clock in the morning" courage. They aren't frightened by nightmares, ghosts or shadows.

155. COMMAND AND CONTROL

To DEFEAT McCLELLAN, LEE HAD DEVISED A BRILLIANT plan. Stonewall Jackson's division would "advance at 3 a.m. on the 26th" and turn the Union right flank. Then the divisions of A. P. Hill, D. (Daniel) H. Hill and Longstreet would move out. "The four divisions keeping in communication with each other, and moving in echelon on separate roads" would then close "upon the enemy's rear." If the Union army began a general retreat, the two Confederate divisions manning the Richmond defenses would join in a vigorous pursuit of the fleeing enemy.

Jackson never showed up on the 26th. He got lost along the way. As Walter Taylor recalled:

It was a remarkable fact that . . . the Confederates were operating to the greatest disadvantage because of their ignorance of the country and the lack of accurate maps showing its topography and the location of the roads.

Lee's division commanders waited twelve hours. Then, hearing nothing from Jackson, A. P. Hill attacked, as he later explained, "rather than hazard the failure of the whole plan by longer deferring it." In the battle of Mechanicsville that followed, the Union troops maintained their positions and inflicted over 1,400 casualties on the attacking Confederates, four times as many as their own losses.

ADVICE

Dwight D. Eisenhower said, "Before the battle is joined planning is everything. After the battle is joined, plans are worthless." The most brilliant plan will not lead to success if your organization lacks effective command and control mechanisms. Rarely are we able to implement complex plans without modification. The people responsible for executing the plans need to be in constant contact so that any difficulties or delays are promptly communicated. Plans often have to be revised on the fly, but unless the total picture is clear to all of the managers responsible for their implementation, the revisions will be piecemeal, disjointed and unsuccessful.

156. DON'T BROOK INTERFERENCE

*D*URING THE BATTLE OF MECHANICSVILLE, JEFFERSON Davis came out to the battlefield with an entourage. At the battle of Seven Pines, Lee had watched Davis issue orders for troop movements to General Johnston's subordinates. Wanting to make sure that Davis wouldn't repeat that mistake, Lee rode over and addressed him in a less than friendly manner:

Who are all this army of people and what are they doing here?

It is not my army, General.

It is certainly not my army, Mr. President, and this is no place for it.

Well, General, if I withdraw, perhaps they will follow me.

ADVICE

Your boss should be kept informed and has every right to see what's happening, but a meddlesome boss needs to be reminded that only you should be giving direct orders to your subordinates.

157. SPILT MILK

*I*N SPITE OF HIS VICTORY AT MECHANICSVILLE, McClellan withdrew, and the following day, Lee won his first battle at Gaines' Mill. McClellan was now in full retreat. Over the next three days (June 28–30), Lee tried to catch his fleeing foe. A. L. Long remembered that, after the battle of Gaines' Mill, Lee ordered General Magruder

to keep a vigilant watch on the Federals and without delay report any movement that might be discovered. These instructions were not as faithfully executed as they should have been, for the retreat of the Federals had commenced on the 28th, and was not discovered until the morning of the 29th, when the Federal lines were found . . . to be abandoned.

While an opportunity had been lost on the 28th, if Magruder could attack McClellan's rearguard on the 29th and slow down the Union retreat, Lee could still trap McClellan's army on the 30th. Lee sent the following order to Magruder:

In order to reap the fruit of our victory the pursuit should be most vigorous. I must urge you, then, again to press on his rear rapidly and steadily. We must lose no more time or he will escape us entirely.

A D V I C E

There is no point in crying over spilt milk. A missed opportunity doesn't mean you have to lose the ball game. It just means you have to play catch up.

*A*s a cadet at West Point, McClellan had been president of the Napoleon Club. He rather enjoyed being called "the little Napoleon." Certainly he seems to have taken to heart a comment by Voltaire, but one usually attributed to Napoleon, "God is always on the side of the big battalions."

At the battle of Gaines' Mill on June 27th, the Confederates had dislodged the Union troops, who withdrew from their positions in good order after inflicting nearly 9,000 casualties on the Confederates while sustaining just under 7,000 themselves. After the battle, McClellan sent the following telegram to Edwin M. Stanton, the U. S. Secretary of War:

Had I 20,000 or even 10,000 fresh troops to use tomorrow, I could take Richmond; but I have not a man in reserve, and shall be glad to cover my retreat and save the material and personnel of the army. . . . I have lost this battle because my force was too small. . . . I know that a few thousand men more would have changed this battle from a defeat to a victory.

Angry that he had not received the reinforcements he had requested, McClellan added, "If I save this army now, I tell you plainly that I owe no thanks to you or to any other persons in Washington. You have done your best to sacrifice this army."

ADVICE

Some managers have an insatiable appetite for scarce resources, and are quick to lay the blame for their failures on their superiors for not giving them everything they want. They make the mistake of believing that their effectiveness as managers is directly proportional to the size of their organization.

*M*AGRUDER DID ATTACK THE UNION REARGUARD AT Savage's Station on June 29th, but was unsuccessful in slowing McClellan's retreat. Lee's last opportunity to catch McClellan in mid-flight and to envelop and destroy his army came the following day at White Oak Swamp. His plan called for six divisions to converge upon McClellan's retreating soldiers.

In the ensuing battle (Frayser's Farm or Glendale), three divisions failed to engage the enemy, and the Confederate forces that were engaged were insufficient to trap McClellan's army, which successfully continued its retreat. In his report of the battle, Lee stated, "Could the other commands have cooperated in the action the result would have proved most disastrous to the enemy." A. L. Long believed the failure to achieve a complete victory was "the result of inattention to orders and want of proper energy on the part of a few subordinate commanders." However, it is also necessary to remember that the envelopment Lee's plan called for was a very complex operation, involving a high degree of coordination among men who had only been working together for a short time.

ADVICE

Even the best laid plans will not succeed if your subordinates fail to carry them out. It makes no sense to develop plans that require skills, coordination or judgment that your people, due to inexperience or insufficient training, do not yet possess. When bringing units together that have not worked with each other previously, you need to be careful to keep the plans as simple and unambiguous as possible.

160. DELEGATE, DON'T ABDICATE

*W*HEN GENERAL JUBAL A. EARLY REMARKED THAT IT looked like McClellan might make good his escape, Lee replied, "Yes, he will get away because I cannot have my orders carried out." Later in the war, Lee told a German observer that his directing a battle personally "would do more harm than good," and that he needed to rely on his "brigade and division commanders."

I strive to make my plans as good as my human skills allow, but on the day of battle I lay the fate of my army in the hands of God; it is my generals' turn to perform their duty.

General E. P. Alexander believed that Lee's leadership style was to some degree responsible for the Confederate failure to destroy McClellan's army on June 30th.

Yet it is hardly correct . . . to say that the failure to reap the greatest result was in no way General Lee's fault. No commander of any army does his whole duty who simply gives orders, however well considered. He should supervise their execution . . . constantly, day and night, so that if the machine balks at any point, he may be most promptly informed and may most promptly start it to work. For instance on June 30 I think he should have been . . . receiving reports every half hour or oftener, and giving fresh orders as needed.

ADVICE

The difference between delegation and effective delegation is follow-up. After you've explained to your subordinates what you want, why you want it, and by when you want it, you can't sit back, put your feet up on your desk and take a nap. You have to begin actively checking on progress and helping your subordinates around any stumbling blocks they encounter.

161. CONCENTRATE YOUR RESOURCES

ON JULY 1ST, THE CONFEDERATES FOUND MCCLELLAN in a very strong defensive position on Malvern Hill. Union artillery commanded the exposed slopes. Lee planned a massive artillery barrage that was to be followed by an infantry attack. The Confederate artillery was ineffective, and the attack that followed was a disaster. As D. H. Hill recalled:

> As each brigade emerged from the woods, from 50 to 100 guns opened upon it, tearing great gaps in its ranks. . . . It was not war, it was murder.

The failed assault cost Lee's army over 5,000 casualties. On Malvern Hill, the Union army had massed 100 guns, and had another 150 in reserve. Lee's order for the battle began with the following sentence: "Batteries have been established to rake the enemy's lines." However, at this stage in the war, each Confederate brigade had its own artillery, and, as one man recalled, "there was nowhere any authority to bring these scattered batteries together and make them effective by massing them." During the course of the day, probably no more than twenty guns ever fired simultaneously at the Union position. The Union gunners responded by concentrating their enormous firepower on each Confederate battery in turn, and quickly put all of them out of action.

ADVICE

Effective leaders are able to concentrate their resources and bring them to bear on the desired objective.

162. IF YOU THINK YOU'RE WHIPPED

*A*FTER WINNING THE BATTLE OF MALVERN HILL, McClellan, instead of following up on his victory, retreated to Harrison's Landing on the James River where his army was under the protection of Union gunboats.

At Mechanicsville and Malvern Hill, the first and the last engagements of the Seven Days, the Union army had won overwhelming victories. When the week had started, McClellan's army outnumbered Lee's by a margin of five to four. The battles of the Seven Days had resulted in over 20,000 Confederate casualties. Union losses were just under 16,000. Thus, as Walter Taylor recalled, "when McClellan reached the river with eighty-five or ninety thousand men, he was being pursued by General Lee with but sixty-two thousand." In spite of his victories and his numerical superiority, McClellan's dispatches reveal that he was a beaten man.

I dread the result if we are attacked today by fresh troops. . . . I now pray for time.

ADVICE

If you think you can't, you're right.

Napoleon said, "The personality of the general is indispensable . . . he is the all of an army."

163. OVERANXIOUS

$\mathcal{O}$N THE MORNING OF JULY 3RD, JEB STUART'S CAVALRY found that the Union army had retreated to Harrison's Landing on the James River. However, McClellan had failed to occupy Evelington Heights, which overlooked the Union camp. If the Confederates could seize and fortify these heights, their artillery could rain destruction down upon the Union army. Instead of waiting quietly for rein-forcements to come up and secure the heights, Stuart decided to use his cavalry's single howitzer to fire on the Union camp. As he later reported, "Judging from the great commotion and excitement caused below, it must have had considerable effect."

Stuart's cannonade awakened the Union commanders to the potential danger, and Union infantry were dispatched to gain possession of the heights and strongly fortify them. The next day, McClellan reported:

We now occupy Evelington Heights. . . . These heights command our whole position, and must be maintained.

ADVICE

Don't be overanxious. Prematurely seizing an opportunity can be worse than not seizing it at all.

At the end of the Seven Days campaign, Lee congratulated his army.

The battle beginning on the afternoon of the 26th of June . . . continued until the night of July 1st, with only such intervals as were necessary to pursue and overtake the flying foe. . . . The immediate fruits of our success are the relief of Richmond from a state of siege; the rout of the great army that so long menaced its safety.

However, Lee told his wife, "Our success has not been so great or complete as we could have desired." In his formal report he wrote:

Under ordinary circumstances the Federal Army should have been destroyed. . . . But regret that more was not accomplished gives way to gratitude to the Sovereign Ruler of the Universe for the results achieved. . . . More than ten thousand prisoners including officers of rank, fifty-two pieces of artillery, and upwards of thirty-five thousand stand of small arms were captured. The stores and supplies of every description which fell into our hands were great in amount and value.

As his son, Rob, recalled, Lee's "great victory did not elate him."

His was a practical, every-day religion which supported him all through his life, enabled him to bear with equanimity every reverse of fortune, and to accept her gifts without undue elation.

ADVICE

Even for great leaders, complete and total triumphs are rare. We need to move from one incomplete victory to another, being careful not to be elated by success or disheartened by failure. The life of a leader is, according to Theodore Roosevelt, "one long campaign where every victory merely leaves the ground free for another battle."

CONTINUOUS
IMPROVEMENT

July 1862–January 1863

After his victory in the battles of the Seven Days, Lee takes a number of steps to improve the performance of his army. The value of these is apparent at the second battle of Manassas (Bull Run), where he is victorious. However, his first invasion of the North ends in failure, when he withdraws to Virginia after the battle of Antietam (Sharpsburg). In December, he inflicts another defeat upon the Union army at the battle of Fredericksburg. When one of his brothers compliments him on his successes, Lee responds:

I am glad you derive satisfaction from the operations
of the army. I acknowledge nothing can surpass
the valor and endurance of our troops, yet while
so much remains to be done, I feel as if nothing
had been accomplished. But we must endure to the end,
and if our people are true to themselves . . . I have no
fear of the result. We may be annihilated,
but we cannot be conquered.

165. WEED YOUR GARDEN

*A*FTER THE BATTLES OF THE SEVEN DAYS, LEE BEGAN to reorganize his army. His failure to destroy McClellan's army had been due to a number of factors, but Lee believed that chief among these was that several of his division commanders had not carried out his orders. Three of them were transferred out of the Army of Northern Virginia. As Lee explained to Jefferson Davis:

> *This army is improving, increasing, reorganizing, and undergoing daily instruction. When we get the new officers in their places, I mean the present vacancies filled, their improvement will be more apparent. I need not tell you that the whole division takes tone from its commander. The brigade receives its share in addition to what is imparted from the brigadier.*

ADVICE

The influence a person exerts on an organization increases geometrically as he or she ascends the management ladder. The removal of ineffective higher level managers from your organization needs to be a top priority.

166. BALANCE STAFF AND LINE

*L*EE WAS RELUCTANT TO BUILD UP STAFF AT THE expense of the line. In response to War Department orders transferring 23 privates to "duty in commissary, ordnance, and medical departments," Lee wrote the Secretary of War:

> *I fear that both officers and men are assigned to special duty . . . in which the public service is not sufficiently considered. Efforts are constantly made to release men from the ranks where they are most needed.*

A D V I C E

Bloated staff departments have been the death of many a good company. You want yours to be as lean as possible while still being able to function effectively. The best way to insure that you will strike the proper balance between staff and line is to have staff department managers who understand that they are there to support line operations, rather than suck the lifeblood from them.

167. BLOWHARDS

ON JULY 14, 1862, THE NEW UNION FIELD COMMANDER, General John Pope, issued the following order:

I have come from the West, where we have always seen the backs of our enemies—from an army whose business it has been to seek the adversary and beat him when found. . . . I desire you to dismiss from your minds certain phrases which I am sorry to find much in vogue amongst you. I constantly hear of taking strong positions and holding them—of lines of retreat and bases of supplies. Let us dismiss such ideas. The strongest position a soldier should desire to occupy is one from which he can most easily advance against the enemy.

In mid-August, Pope realized that he had marched into a potential trap. His army was in a triangle formed by the Rapidan and Rappahannock Rivers, and would almost certainly be wiped out if the Confederates were to attack while it was in that position. Pope, quite sensibly, retreated, but in doing so, he exposed himself to criticism for adopting one of those "lines of retreat" which he had told his officers and men to dismiss from their minds.

ADVICE

Avoid grandiose predictions. They can make you look like a fool to those who realize how difficult it may be to keep them, and, should you fail, make your fall from grace even greater for those who believed you.

168. GAIN YOUR BOSS' CONFIDENCE

THE DAY AFTER GIVING LEE COMMAND OF THE ARMY of Northern Virginia, Davis had made the following request: "Please keep me advised as frequently as your engagements will permit of what is passing before and around you."

In August 1862, Lee moved his headquarters to northern Virginia to meet the threat from General Pope. Realizing the Confederate President would be concerned that Lee's absence from Richmond would mean the end of the close personal contact they had enjoyed, Lee told Davis not to worry:

I will keep you informed of everything of importance that transpires. When you do not hear from me, you may feel sure that I do not think it necessary to trouble you. I shall be obliged to you for any directions you may think proper to give.

General Johnston recognized the important advantage that Lee had in having Jefferson Davis' confidence. When a friend expressed concern for the South now that Johnston was out of the action, Johnston replied:

The shot that struck me down is the very best that has been fired for the Southern cause yet. For I possess in no degree the confidence of our government, and now they have in my place one who does possess it, and who can accomplish what I never could have done.

ADVICE

If you don't have your boss' confidence, he or she will be constantly breathing down your neck. You'll never have any peace, and you'll find it difficult, if not impossible, to do your job. A prerequisite to getting your boss to trust you is to keep him or her informed. No one likes surprises. Keeping your boss posted regularly should make it easier for him or her to swallow the bad news that you will on occasion have to deliver.

169. FIGHT FIRE WITH FIRE

*W*HEN UNION SOLDIERS BEGAN ARRESTING AND
threatening Confederate civilians, Lee wrote to General
McClellan:

> *This Government refuses to admit the right of the*
> *authorities of the United States to arrest our citizens and*
> *extort from them their parole not to render military service*
> *to their country. . . . Should your Government treat . . .*
> *such service by these persons as a breach of parole and*
> *punish it accordingly this Government will resort to retalia-*
> *tory measures as the only means of compelling the obser-*
> *vance of the rules of civilized warfare.*

When Lee learned that a Union general had threatened to kill civilians in retaliation for guerrilla activity, he
replied that he would immediately hang a captured Union
officer for each murdered civilian. As Lee explained, he
would wage "war on the terms chosen by our enemies until
the voice of an outraged humanity shall compel a respect
for the recognized usages of war."

ADVICE

Your organization's success depends upon your ability and
willingness to take the steps that are needed to level the
playing field, especially when dealing with foreign competitors.

170. THE PETER PRINCIPLE

*D*URING THE SEVEN DAYS, LEE FELT THAT D. H. HILL had done a good job as a division commander. After the battles, he was given command of the Department of North Carolina. His primary responsibility was to harass McClellan, who was camped at Harrison's Landing. On August 2, 1862, Lee wrote to Hill:

I am glad to learn . . . that your attack upon the enemy's shipping was successful. . . . But this does not satisfy the object I had in view. My desire was for you to cut off their communication by the river. . . . This will require continuous and systematic effort and a well digested plan.

Five days later, Lee wrote again to Hill: "I regret to hear of the feeble conduct of your cavalry. . . . I hope you will lose no opportunity of damaging the enemy in every way." On August 17th, Lee learned that McClellan had escaped. Believing that McClellan "ought not to have got off so easily," Lee told Jefferson Davis:

I fear General [D. H.] Hill is not entirely equal to his present position . . . . Left to himself he seems embarrassed and backward to act.

On the basis of Lee's recommendation, Hill was relieved of command for the department and resumed his position as one of the army's division commanders.

A D V I C E

People who fail after being promoted deserve your help. You promoted them because they had been superior performers in their prior positions. The fault for their failure is partially yours for putting them in jobs for which they are not suited, and it is your responsibility to get them back into jobs in which they can again perform well. When McClellan got away from D. H. Hill, Lee wrote: "I fear all was not done that might have been done to harass and destroy our enemies, but I blame nobody but myself."

171. START THE BALL ROLLING

*C*ONVINCED THAT MCCLELLAN WAS MOVING TO JOIN forces with Pope, Lee gave orders for the movement of his entire army to northern Virginia. As he explained to President Davis:

> *The whole army I think should be united here as soon as possible. I have ordered up [General Roswell S.] Ripley . . . and will direct General G. [Gustavus] W. Smith to send on [Lafayette] McLaws, D. H. Hill and other available troops. Should you not agree with me in the propriety of this step please countermand the order and let me know.*

ADVICE

When speed is of the essence, and you are convinced that you know what steps need to be taken, don't hesitate to get the ball rolling. Let your boss know what you are doing. If your boss agrees with the actions you've initiated, you're ahead of the game; if not, very little has been lost.

172. CONTINUOUS IMPROVEMENT

*H*AVING FAILED TO CATCH POPE'S ARMY NORTH OF THE Rappahannock River, Lee dispatched Stonewall Jackson to circle around the Union army and capture its main supply base at Manassas Junction. Jackson did this on August 27, 1862. For the next two days, he held off Pope, while Lee and Longstreet moved into position to attack the Union army's left flank. On August 30th, after the second battle of Manassas (Bull Run), Lee telegraphed Davis:

This army achieved today on the plains of Manassas a signal victory over the combined forces of Generals McClellan and Pope.

Lee had defeated Pope's larger army and sent it high-tailing back to the safety of Washington. Lee's reorganization had begun to pay dividends. Both planning and execution had been considerably better than in the battles of the Seven Days in which Confederate casualties had been greater than those sustained by the Union. At Second Manassas, Confederate casualties were less than 10,000, while the Union losses numbered 16,000.

ADVICE

Executives who talk about wanting their organizations to be "best in class" are missing the point. Being the best only means that you are better than your current competitors. Continuous improvement is required to stay ahead of the competition. Never let "best" become the enemy of "better."

173. CREEPING INSUBORDINATION

*L*ONGSTREET HAD REACHED THE BATTLEFIELD ON August 29th. Lee wanted him to attack immediately, but Longstreet wanted to examine the ground first. Lee agreed to wait. Later in the day, he asked Longstreet, "Hadn't we better move our line forward?" Longstreet, believing that he needed additional information on enemy troop movements before committing his forces, answered, "I think not." Toward evening, Lee again tried to get him to attack, but as Longstreet recalled:

> *I suggested that, the day being far spent, it might be well to advance before night on a forced reconnaissance, get our troops in the most favorable positions, and have all things ready for battle the next morning.*

Lee reluctantly agreed. While some historians think that had Longstreet attacked Pope's left flank on the 29th, the Union army might have been destroyed, others believe no harm was done by waiting until the following day. The real damage was to the relationship between Lee and Longstreet. After Second Manassas, Longstreet seemed to think that if he simply dug his heels in and hung tough, he could always have his way.

ADVICE

Nothing is more dangerous than subordinates who have come to believe that, if they continue to insist on their preferred alternative, you will eventually give in and let them have their way. This doesn't mean that you don't want input from your staff, or that on occasion they may raise objections that cause you to alter your plans. However, once you've made your decision, you need to give crisp orders, not suggestions or recommendations, that clearly spell out what you want and by when you want it. Your subordinates need to understand that your directions must be carried out with competence, enthusiasm and dispatch.

*W*HILE WAITING FOR LONGSTREET TO ATTACK, THE tension among Lee's staff had been intense. If the Union troops had broken Jackson's line before Longstreet went into action, it could have meant defeat and even disaster. As one Confederate officer recalled, "Everybody's nerves were at the tensest—everybody's except General Lee's. His countenance did not show the least excitement or concern." Noticing some mule-drawn wagons, Lee told one of his officers:

I observe that some of those mules are without shoes. I wish you would see to it that all of the animals are shod at once.

Lee knew that the army depended upon wagons for transport, and unshod mules would break down more quickly than properly shod animals. It was too important a detail to overlook regardless of what else was happening.

A D V I C E

Even at times of great stress, when you need to focus your attention on the big picture, you cannot afford to overlook the critical details which, if not attended to, can upset your plans.

Good leaders remain outwardly calm and unemotional even under the most stressful conditions. By their example, they set the tone for their subordinates.

 175. SINGLE-MINDEDNESS

*A*FTER HE LEARNED OF STONEWALL JACKSON'S successful raid on his supply depot, General Pope seemed to become obsessed with destroying Jackson. He ignored warnings that Lee and Longstreet were coming to Jackson's assistance. On the morning of August 30th, after two days of hard fighting, Pope sent the following message:

> *We fought a terrific battle here yesterday . . . which lasted with continuous fury from daybreak until dark, by which time the enemy was driven from the field. . . . Our troops are too much exhausted yet to push matters, but I shall do so in the course of the morning. . . . The enemy is still in our front, but badly used up. We have lost not less than 8,000 men killed and wounded.*

Pope seemed oblivious to the fact that Longstreet with 30,000 fresh troops was now poised on the left flank of the Union army.

ADVICE

Don't become so obsessed with accomplishing one goal that you get blindsided, because your attention has been so narrowly focused. The single-minded pursuit of a goal to the exclusion of everything else is folly.

*P*OPE'S ARMY WAS ABLE TO SUCCESSFULLY RETREAT after being defeated at Second Manassas because the Confederates were in no condition to pursue. Lee later explained, "My men had nothing to eat. . . . They had had nothing to eat for three days." On the day of the battle, he had written to Jefferson Davis, "Beef, flour and forage may be obtained . . . by proper exertions in the different depart- ments." But the "proper exertions" were not made, and throughout the war, Lee's movements were hamstrung by the lack of supplies. As A. L. Long recalled:

The abundant supplies with which the country teemed at the beginning of the war, instead of being collected and reserved for future use, were allowed to be dissipated.

Lee made repeated requests for food and clothing for his army. After the winter of 1862–1863, during which his men had suffered terribly due to the lack of food and equipment, Lee wrote to the Secretary of War:

The troops . . . have for some time been confined to reduced rations. . . . Symptoms of scurvy are appearing among them, and to supply the place of vegetables each regiment is directed to send a daily detail to gather sas- safras buds, wild onions, lamb's quarter, and poke sprouts.

I have understood, I do not know with what truth, that the Army of the West and that in the Department of South Carolina and Georgia are more bountifully supplied with provisions. . . . I think this army deserves as much consideration as either of those named, and if it can be supplied, respectfully ask that it be similarly provided.

During the winter of 1863–1864, Lee received a letter from one of his soldiers who said the men would manage on short rations if necessary, but he wondered if Lee knew how little they had to eat. Lee wrote to the Commissary General, "I have been mortified to find that when any scarcity existed this was the only army in which it is found necessary to reduce the rations."

It wasn't until February 1865, two months before he surrendered at Appomattox, that Lee told the Secretary of War:

If some change is not made and the Commissary Department reorganized, I apprehend dire results. The physical strength of the men . . . must fail under this treatment. . . . You must not be surprised if calamity befalls us.

In the summer of 1862, when Lee first realized that the Commissary Department was being mismanaged, he should have insisted that Davis replace the head of the department with a more competent officer.

ADVICE

A British observer with Lee's army wrote that Lee's "only faults . . . arise from his excessive amiability." You want to be polite, but there are instances when you have to take your gloves off and be forceful and direct. You can only wait so long for politeness to work before insisting that corrective action be taken.

ON SEPTEMBER 3, 1862, LEE PROPOSED TO INVADE THE North, but as he explained to President Davis:

The army is not properly equipped for an invasion of the enemy's territory. It lacks much of the material of war, is feeble in transportation, the animals being much reduced, and the men are poorly provided with clothes, and in thousands of instances are destitute of shoes.

Lee had waited nearly a month before beginning offensive operations at the start of the Seven Days. During that time he had instructed his subordinates to "be careful to preserve their men as much as possible, that they may be fresh when called upon for active service." Now, only one week after his victory at Second Manassas, he was marching his hungry, tired and shoeless army into harm's way. A Maryland man, who watched them pass, recalled:

I know something of the appearance of a marching army, both Union and Southern. There are always stragglers, of course, but never before or after did I see anything comparable to the demoralized state of the Confederates at this time. Never were want and exhaustion more visibly put before my eyes.

The number of men that dropped out of the ranks was so alarming that on September 13th Lee informed Davis, "Our ranks are very much diminished. I fear from a third to a half of the original numbers." Four days later at Antietam (Sharpsburg), Lee would fight a Union army nearly twice the size of his own.

ADVICE

If you know better, don't do it.

178. NEGOTIATE FROM A POSITION OF STRENGTH

*W*ITH TWO RECENT VICTORIES UNDER HIS BELT, VIRGINIA virtually free of Union troops, and his army marching into Maryland, Lee proposed to Jefferson Davis that the Confederacy offer to begin peace negotiations.

Such a proposition coming from us at this time, could in no way be regarded as suing for peace; but, being made when it is in our power to inflict injury upon our adversary, would show conclusively to the world that our sole object is the establishment of our independence and the attainment of an honorable peace. The rejection of this offer would prove to the country that the responsibility of the continuance of this war does not rest upon us. . . . The proposal of peace would enable the people of the United States to determine at their coming elections whether they will support those who favor a prolongation of the war, or those who wish to bring it to a termination.

A D V I C E

The best time to offer to negotiate is when you can do so from a position of strength.

179. WHEN THE LEOPARD CHANGES HIS SPOTS

*A*FTER HE CROSSED THE POTOMAC RIVER, LEE DIVIDED his army. The largest force under Jackson would capture Martinsburg, West Virginia and the Union garrison at Harpers Ferry. Then the army would reunite and march on Harrisburg, Pennsylvania. When one of his brigadiers expressed astonishment at so daring a plan, Lee asked him if he was acquainted with General McClellan.

He is an able general, but a very cautious one. . . . His army . . . will not be prepared for offensive operations—or he will not think it so—for three or four weeks. Before that time I hope to be on the Susquehanna.

Suddenly McClellan began to advance rapidly and purposefully to drive a wedge between Lee's divided army. Lee realized that McClellan was acting like a changed man. He reacted to McClellan's changed behavior by ordering the army to retreat to Sharpsburg, Maryland, preparatory to re-crossing the Potomac into Virginia.

A D V I C E

When your competitor begins acting out of character, you need to step back and reassess the situation. Try to figure out what has caused the change in behavior and whether it is a temporary aberration or likely to be permanent.

An extra copy of Lee's plan for the march through Maryland had been used by one of D. H. Hill's staff officers as wrapping paper for three of his cigars. He must have dropped the cigars and their wrapping because they were found by Union soldiers and delivered to General McClellan. When the handwriting established that the order was genuine, McClellan exclaimed:

Here is a paper with which if I cannot whip Bobby Lee, I will be willing to go home.

McClellan telegraphed President Lincoln:

I have the whole rebel force in front of me, but am confident, and no time shall be lost. . . . I have all the plans of the rebels, and will catch them in their own trap.

ADVICE

No one likes a clean desk policy. It is an awful nuisance to have to lock everything up at the end of each day. But nothing else works. Confidential documents must be secured; otherwise you run the risk of revealing your organization's secrets.

Longstreet, in order to be certain that his copy of Lee's order could not fall into enemy hands, chewed it up.

181. REMEMBER YOUR PURPOSE

On the morning of September 15th, the Union garrison at Harpers Ferry surrendered to Jackson. As Lee later reported, "Leaving A. P. Hill to receive the surrender of the Federal troops and secure the captured property, General Jackson, with his two other divisions, set out at once for Sharpsburg" where Lee had taken up defensive positions.

Early on the morning of the 17th, McClellan attacked. During the course of that long day, the single bloodiest of the war, Lee's men successively repulsed attacks against their left, their center and their right. The final Union attack was broken by the timely arrival of A. P. Hill's division, which had left Harpers Ferry that morning and marched the 17 miles to the battlefield.

Although McClellan enjoyed nearly two-to-one numerical superiority, he employed only about one-half of his force during the battle. He was urged by his subordinates to bring some of the men he was holding in reserve into action, but he refused. Had he committed the bulk of his army, there is little doubt that the Confederates would have been overwhelmed.

McClellan seemed to have forgotten that his objective was the destruction of Lee's army. Lincoln had not forgotten that. He was furious with McClellan and, later that year, relieved him of command.

ADVICE

There are always risks associated with committing your resources, but you must be willing to take them. Your mission is not to conserve your resources but to use them wisely to accomplish your goals.

Lee was sorry to see McClellan replaced. He told Longstreet, "We always understood each other so well. I fear they may continue to make these changes till they find someone whom I don't understand."

182. ROLL UP YOUR SLEEVES AND DO REAL WORK

$\mathcal{D}$URING THE BATTLE OF ANTIETAM (SHARPSBURG), AS units became disorganized and their officers were killed or wounded, a number of senior officers found that they needed to perform duties normally assigned to their juniors. General Longstreet held the horses of his aides while they fired two cannon. Lee personally directed the movement of troops on the field. Late in the day, he directed the fire of an artillery battery, something he had not done since the Mexican War. The lieutenant commanding the battery, concerned for Lee's safety, immediately protested: "General Lee, as soon as we fire we will draw the enemy's fire." Lee told him, "Never mind me," and ordered him to open fire.

ADVICE

Occasionally, you have to go down into the trenches and do work that is normally assigned to your subordinates. Good leaders don't hesitate to do so when necessary. However, if "when necessary" becomes a routine occurrence, that's a sure sign of management failure.

183. SPIN

 $\mathcal{T}$ HE CONFEDERATES HAD SUFFERED OVER 10,000 casualties (one quarter of Lee's army) at Sharpsburg. On the night of September 17th, all of his generals favored an immediate retreat. Lee, wanting to collect his stragglers and move his wounded to safety, decided to stay put. One of his officers remembered him saying:

Gentlemen, we will not cross the Potomac tonight. . . . If McClellan wants to fight in the morning, I will give him battle again.

McClellan had no interest in fighting the following day. As he explained:

After a night of anxious deliberation. . . . I concluded that the success of an attack on the 18th was not certain.

Lee reported to President Davis that "finding the enemy indisposed to make an attack" after nightfall on the 18th, he withdrew across the Potomac to the Virginia side. Lee's first invasion of the North had ended in failure, but, by refusing to accept Lee's challenge to renew the battle, McClellan had given the Confederates the perception of at least a partial victory. Lee issued the following order to his army:

On the field of Sharpsburg, with less than one-third his numbers, you resisted from daylight until dark the whole army of the enemy, and repulsed every attack. . . . The whole of the following day you stood prepared to resume the conflict on the same ground, and retired next morning without molestation across the Potomac. . . .

History records fewer examples of greater fortitude and endurance than this army has exhibited, and I am commissioned by the President to thank you in the name of the Confederate States for the undying fame you have won.

A D V I C E

Perception can be more important than reality. Good leaders pay as much attention to how their actions are perceived as they do to what they accomplish.

LEE HAD RECOGNIZED THAT CROSSING INTO MARYLAND was a move "attended with much risk." He was thinking of the military risk. Jefferson Davis should have been thinking of the larger political risk. McClellan had not won a battlefield victory, but less than two weeks after invading Maryland, Lee had retreated to Virginia, and that was a strategic defeat.

After Lee's victory at Second Manassas, in response to a query from the Prime Minister, the British Foreign Secretary had written:

I agree with you that the time has come for offering mediation to the United States Government, with a view to recognition of the independence of the Confederates. I agree further that, in case of failure, we ought ourselves to recognize the Southern States as an independent State.

After learning of Lee's advance into Maryland, the Prime Minister replied:

It is evident that a great conflict is taking place to the northwest of Washington. . . . If the Federals sustain a grave defeat, they may be at once ready for mediation. . . . If, on the other hand, they should have the best of it, we may wait a while and see what may follow.

Lee's withdrawal was a victory for the Union. On September 22, 1862, Abraham Lincoln told his cabinet, "When the rebel army was at Frederick, I determined, as soon as it should be driven out of Maryland, to issue a proclamation of emancipation." Once the abolition of slavery became a goal of the Union war effort, given the political realities in Britain and France, there was no longer any serious possibility of European intervention in America's Civil War.

ADVICE

Your actions need to be viewed in terms of their potential impact on the larger picture. A well-publicized failure, even one that does little real harm to a company's results or prospects, can do incalculable harm in the minds of analysts, investors, the press and the public.

185. PROMOTIONS

*A*FTER RETURNING TO VIRGINIA, LEE FORMALLY reorganized his army into two corps, one under Longstreet and the other under Jackson. Both men were promoted to lieutenant general.

The promotions of Longstreet and Jackson created two vacancies, but Lee made no recommendation regarding their replacements. He wrote to Jefferson Davis:

I believe you have sufficient names before you to fill the vacancies. Your own knowledge of the claims and qualifications of the officers will, I feel assured, enable you to make the best selection.

Even if Davis made excellent selections, it was wrong for Lee to ask him to fill the openings instead of making the promotions himself.

ADVICE

There is no responsibility more important than the selection of managers. You are accountable for their performance. You are also the most qualified to make the selection. You want to consult their current and former managers, your peers and your boss, but only you should make the decision. When one of your managers recommends someone for promotion, you have an obligation to satisfy yourself that he or she has selected a worthy candidate, but you should never take the decision out of your manager's hands and make it yourself.

186. NO, BECAUSE

*I*N NOVEMBER 1862, JEB STUART SUGGESTED A movement by the army. In rejecting the proposal, Lee pointed out that it wouldn't be wise to let the Union army take a position

between Jackson's and Longstreet's corps, which would be the case, if the movement you suggested was made.

ADVICE

The word "no" should be used sparingly, and never without giving a reason. "Because I said so" and "because we've always done it this way" are not valid reasons.

187. BUILD IN A CUSHION

*W*HEN LEE REALIZED THAT THE NEW COMMANDER of the Union Army of the Potomac, General Ambrose E. Burnside, was concentrating on the north bank of the Rappahannock River opposite Fredericksburg, he wrote to Stonewall Jackson to alert him.

I will advise you from time to time of the movements of the enemy and of mine . . . but you must make allowances for the inaccuracy of the first and the delay of the second, and predicate your movements so as to be on the safe side.

ADVICE

You need to build a cushion and safeguards into your plans.

188. BE CAREFUL OF WHAT YOU ASK FOR

*T*HE NEW COMMANDER OF THE UNION ARMY OF THE Potomac, General Burnside, had put in motion a plan to advance on Richmond by way of Fredericksburg. At first, everything went according to plan, but then the pontoons needed for bridging the Rappahannock were late. While Burnside sat and waited for their arrival, Lee united his army and took up virtually impregnable positions on the other side of the river. Union infantry would have to cross an open plain that was commanded by 300 Confederate cannon. E. P. Alexander told Longstreet:

We cover that ground so well that we will comb it as with a fine-tooth comb. A chicken could not live on that field when we open on it.

McClellan had been fired for being too cautious. Lincoln wanted the Army of the Potomac to fight, and Burnside was afraid of the wrath he would incur if he withdrew and sought a more favorable opportunity. He convinced himself that he still had a chance to win. His dispatch to Washington announcing that he had ordered an assault ended with the words, "We hope to succeed."

On December 13, 1862, Burnside hurled his troops in a series of futile charges against the Confederate lines. When Lee expressed concern about the number of Union infantry massing for an attack, Longstreet replied, "General, if you put every man now on the other side of the Potomac in that field . . . and give me plenty of ammunition I will kill them all before they reach my line." Walter Taylor remembered seeing "division after division . . . torn to pieces and driven back." When the day ended, the Union army had suffered nearly 13,000 casualties.

A D V I C E

Be careful of what you demand of your people. Don't push them to the point where they feel the only way they can keep their jobs is to do dumb things.

Burnside, on two previous occasions, had refused an offer to command the Army of the Potomac on the grounds that he did not feel equal to the responsibility. Over his objections, he was ordered to accept the position. It is almost always a mistake to make someone take a job that he or she doesn't feel qualified to perform.

189. COOPERATING WITH THE ENEMY

*W*ATCHING THE AWFUL CARNAGE AT FREDERICKSBURG, Lee remarked, "It is well that war is so terrible—we should grow too fond of it!" There was no action on December 14th, and it wasn't until the afternoon of the 15th, nearly 48 hours after the battle, that Burnside requested a truce so he could collect his dead and wounded. The previous day, as the Union wounded lay in agony on the exposed plain between the two armies, a Confederate sergeant, Richard Kirkland, began bringing water to the wounded. Although Kirkland was plainly visible and within range of their guns, not a single shot was fired at him by Union soldiers.

ADVICE

Not everything your competitors do is bad for you. There are many things you have in common, and on which you can work cooperatively. Civic, legislative and charitable activities provide opportunities for you to unite with your competitors for the common good.

Kirkland was killed at Chickamauga.

190. POSITION YOURSELF FOR THE FUTURE

*L*EE HAD HOPED THAT BURNSIDE WOULD RENEW THE battle, but on the night of December 15th, the Union army retreated. Disappointed, Lee wrote his wife:

> *This morning they were all safe on the north side of the Rappahannock. They went as they came, in the night. They suffered heavily as far as the battle went, but it did not go far enough to satisfy me. . . . The contest will now have to be renewed, but on what field I cannot say.*

The Union army had been able to make a clean getaway because the Confederates had occupied a position that was admirably suited for defense, but provided no opportunity for a counterattack. For this reason Jackson had been opposed to fighting at Fredericksburg. Before the battle, he said, "We will whip the enemy but gain no fruits of victory."

In January 1863, Lee wrote to the Secretary of War:

> *The lives of our soldiers are too precious to be sacrificed in the attainment of successes that inflict no loss upon the enemy beyond the actual loss in battle. Every victory should bring us nearer to the great end which it is the object of this war to reach.*

ADVICE

You need to position yourself so you can capitalize on each success and use it as a stepping stone toward accomplishing your goals.

GATHER INTELLIGENCE. James Ewell Brown (Jeb) Stuart led his cavalry on an intelligence gathering ride around the Union army prior to the start of the battles of the Seven Days. When he rejoined Lee's army, Stuart remarked that he had left a general behind, "General Consternation."

(Virginia Historical Society)

GAIN YOUR BOSS' CONFIDENCE. Relations between Jefferson Davis and two of the Confederacy's five full generals broke down early in the war. Lee gained Davis' confidence by keeping him informed and soliciting his input.

(National Archives)

BLOWHARDS. On assuming command of the Union army in July 1862, General John Pope announced, "My headquarters are in the saddle." Hearing this, Stonewall Jackson said, "I can whip any man that doesn't know his headquarters from his hindquarters."

(National Archives)

CONTINUOUS IMPROVEMENT. Lee and James Longstreet confer during the second battle of Manassas (Bull Run) on August 30, 1862. Lee was able to defeat Pope's larger army because he had used the time between the battles of the Seven Days and Second Manassas to continue to improve the effectiveness of his army.

(Library of Congress)

REMEMBER YOUR PURPOSE. The battlefield at Antietam (Sharpsburg) as seen from the rear of the Union lines. Elements of the Union Fifth Corps, which did not participate in the battle, can be seen in the background. Although his army outnumbered Lee's by two to one, Union General George B. McClellan held half his force in reserve. By being overly cautious, he failed to achieve his objective of destroying Lee's army.

(Library of Congress)

POSITION YOURSELF FOR THE FUTURE. The Union army crossed the Rappahannock and attacked Fredericksburg on December 13, 1862. Lee won a lopsided victory that day, but the positions of the two armies were such that he was unable to counterattack, and the defeated Union army was able to get away safely.

(National Archives)

THE PERFECT COMBINATION. On the night of May 1, 1863, Lee and Thomas J. (Stonewall) Jackson planned the attack that led to the Confederate victory at the battle of Chancellorsville. Jackson was the perfect person to implement Lee's bold plans.

(Battles and Leaders of the Civil War)

IN THE WAKE OF A DISASTER. Lee took full responsibility for the Confederate defeat at Gettysburg. By admitting that he had made a mistake in ordering Pickett's Charge and not faulting the actions of his subordinates, Lee maintained the morale of his army.

(Archive Photos)

DUTY FIRST. When he learned that his nephew, Fitzhugh, was planning a ball, Lee wrote, "I would rather his officers should entertain themselves in fattening their horses, healing their men, and recruiting their regiments.... I like all [the Lees] to be present at battles, but can excuse them at balls."

(Library of Congress)

IF IT'S BROKE, FIX IT. While Union soldiers (shown here) were well fed, Lee was hamstrung by shortages of food for his army. Jefferson Davis waited until February 1865 to address the management problems in the Commissary Department, and by then it was too late.

(U. S. Army Military History Institute)

DO WHAT YOU CAN. Although crippled by arthritis and rheumatism and confined to a wheel chair, Lee's wife, Mary, turned her home into what one observer called an "industrial school." She, her daughters and friends knitted gloves, scarves and socks for the men in Lee's army.

(Valentine Museum, Richmond, Virginia)

SQUEEZE OUT AN EXTRA CONCESSION. At Appomattox (April 9, 1865), Lee received generous terms for the surrender of his army from the Union commander, Ulysses S. Grant. Lee was able to get an additional concession that allowed all of his soldiers, not just the officers, to keep their horses and mules.

(Battles and Leaders of the Civil War)

AN EXPANDING VISION. As president of Washington College, Lee formulated and set about implementing his plans to transform the school into one of "the best institutions in the country." His dynamic and expanding vision for higher education established the model for the modern American university.

(Library of Congress)

RECONCILIATION. After his inauguration as President of the United States on March 4, 1869, Ulysses S. Grant invited Robert E. Lee to the White House. Their meeting on May 1st was an important step on the road to national reconciliation.

(National Archives)

A LASTING LEGACY. Robert E. Lee:
soldier, peacemaker, educator.
(National Archives)

9

THE PERFECT
COMBINATION

January 1863 – April 1864

At Chancellorsville, in May 1863, Lee defeats a Union army that outnumbers his two to one. One of his aides described the scene after the battle as Lee rode to the front:

> *One long, unbroken cheer . . . hailed the presence of the victorious chief. He sat in the full realization of all that soldiers dream of—triumph; and as I looked on him in the complete fruition of the success which his genius, courage and confidence in his army had won, I thought that it must have been from some such scene that men in ancient days ascended to the dignity of gods.*

The death of Stonewall Jackson deprives Lee of his "right arm," and two months later he suffers defeat at Gettysburg. Lee takes full responsibility for the results of the battle. He says, "It's all my fault. I thought my men were invincible." However, the devotion that Lee's soldiers feel for him is not dimmed by the defeat. One of them tells him not to worry: "General, we'll fight them till Hell freezes over, and then we'll fight them on the ice."

191. ADMIRATION AND RESPECT

THE ARMY OF NORTHERN VIRGINIA WAS COMPOSED OF ordinary men who time and again accomplished the seemingly impossible. The admiration and respect they felt for their commander was so great that they would do whatever he asked them to or literally die trying. One soldier described the army's feelings for Lee in these words:

> *We loved him much but revered him more. We never criticized, never doubted him. The proviso with which a ragged rebel accepted the doctrine that "the rest of us may have descended from monkeys, but it took a God to make Marse Robert," had more than mere humor in it. . . . We never compared him with any other men. . . . He was in a superlative and absolute class by himself.*

Senior officers shared these feelings. Stonewall Jackson told an aide, "His perception is as quick and unerring as his judgment is infallible. . . . So great is my confidence in General Lee that I am willing to follow him blindfolded."

ADVICE

Great leaders inspire extraordinary performance. Their people admire and respect them so much that they would do anything rather than disappoint them.

One of Lee's staff was asked, "Does it not make the General proud to see how these men love him?" He replied, "Not proud. It awes him."

192. HERO WORSHIP

*L*EE WAS CONCERNED WITH THE ADULATION HE RECEIVED.

I tremble for my country when I hear of confidence expressed in me. I know too well my own weakness and that our only trust is in God.

ADVICE

There is a fine line between admiration and respect and adulation and hero worship. You want the former but not the latter. There are two obvious dangers with hero worship. If something happens to the leader, and his or her services are lost to the organization, the impact on employee morale and public confidence can be devastating. Good leaders make certain that those inside and outside of the organization understand that the successes that have been achieved are due to the efforts of the senior management team and should not be regarded as the leader's personal triumphs. The other danger is the temptation for the leader to come to believe that he or she really is infallible. Just because your people are willing to try to accomplish the impossible for you doesn't mean that they can do the impossible. Reflecting on his defeat at Gettysburg, Lee wrote, "The army did all it could. I fear I required of it impossibilities."

193. LEAN DOESN'T MEAN EMACIATED

At Fredericksburg, the Confederates had fought from behind fortifications, and Lee had been so pleased with the result that he remarked, "My army is as much stronger for these new entrenchments as if I had received reinforcements of 20,000 men." While fortifications would help to even the odds when his army was operating on the defensive, Lee realized that if he was to achieve a decisive victory, he needed more men. On January 10, 1863, he explained why to the Secretary of War:

The success with which our efforts have been crowned, under the blessing of God, should not betray our people into the dangerous delusion that the armies now in the field are sufficient to bring this war to a successful and speedy conclusion.

While the spirit of our soldiers is unabated, their ranks have been greatly thinned by the casualties of battle and the diseases of the camp. Losses in battle are rendered much heavier by reason of our being compelled to encounter the enemy with inferior numbers. . . .

More than once have most promising opportunities been lost for want of men to take advantage of them.

Lee ended his appeal with the words, "Let every effort be made, every means be employed, to fill and maintain the ranks of our armies, until God, in His mercy, shall bless us with the establishment of our independence." When the Confederate Congress failed to take action, Lee wrote to his son, Custis, "What has our Congress done to meet the exigency, I may say extremity, in which we are placed?" A month before the war ended, he answered his own question by telling Custis that he had "been up to see the Congress and they do not seem to be able to do anything except to eat peanuts and chew tobacco."

A D V I C E

Some managers act as if there is always more fat to be trimmed from their subordinates' operations. They insist on reducing headcount in the face of increasing workloads, even when current opportunities to improve productivity are limited. In your quest to be lean, be wary of becoming so thin that performance suffers.

194. SOUND AND FURY SIGNIFYING NOTHING

THE NEW COMMANDER OF THE UNION ARMY OF THE Potomac was General Joseph Hooker. On February 6, 1863, Lee wrote to his daughter, Agnes:

General Hooker is obliged to do something. I do not know what it will be. . . . He runs out his guns, starts his wagons and troops up and down the river, and creates an excitement generally. Our men look on in wonder, give a cheer, and all again subsides "in statu quo ante bellum."

On April 24th, he wrote his wife:

The enemy is making various demonstrations. . . . Last week they infested all the fords on the upper Rappahannock. . . . Tuesday they abandoned them. Day before yesterday they made their appearance on the lower Rappahannock. Formed in line of battle, threw out skirmishers, advanced their artillery, brought up their wagons, built up large fires, and after dark commenced chopping, cutting and sawing as if working for life till midnight, when the noise ceased and at daylight all had disappeared.

ADVICE

Develop your plans and commit your organization to achieve them. A series of false starts accomplishes nothing. Frustrated by your seeming inability to make up your mind, your people begin to question your competence.

Lee believed that Hooker was being indecisive. He wrote: "I owe . . . Hooker no thanks for keeping me here in this state of expectancy. He ought to have made up his mind long ago what to do."

195. WHAT'S BEST FOR THE
ORGANIZATION

ENERAL LONGSTREET, WITH TWO OF HIS DIVISIONS, HAD been temporarily detached from the Army of Northern Virginia to conduct operations in North Carolina. Without Longstreet, Lee faced a Union army over twice the size of his own. Lee had always given Stonewall Jackson wide latitude when operating independently, because he knew that Jackson placed the army's success ahead of his personal ambition and would promptly rejoin the main body of the army when needed. He gave the same latitude to Longstreet.

I am confident that at all times and in all places you will do all that can be done for the defense of the country and advancement of the service, and are ready to cooperate or act singly as circumstances dictate.

On April 27, 1863, Lee asked Longstreet, "Can you give me any idea when your operations will be completed and whether any of the troops you have in Carolina can be spared from there." Longstreet was lobbying for additional men, and made no effort to send troops to Lee. On the 29th, when he learned that the Union army was crossing the Rappahannock, Lee urgently requested reinforcements. However, his appeal came too late, and Longstreet and his men did not rejoin the army until after the battle of Chancellorsville. While Longstreet's absence did not keep Lee from winning this battle, had Longstreet's divisions been there, Lee might have destroyed the Union army.

ADVICE

It is easy for some people to delude themselves into thinking that what is best for them is also what is best for the organization. Only those subordinates who can differentiate between the two and who place the good of the organization ahead of their personal ambition should be trusted to carry out independent assignments where they will be operating with minimal supervision.

196. THE PERFECT COMBINATION

ENERAL HOOKER'S ARMY BEGAN CROSSING THE Rappahannock on April 29th. His movement was intended to catch Lee's army in a giant pincer. On May 1st, after encountering Confederate resistance near Chancellorsville, Hooker halted his offensive and dug in.

That night Lee determined to send Jackson around the Union army to attack Hooker's exposed right flank. After giving Jackson time to decide how he would make the movement, Lee turned to him and said:

> *General Jackson, what do you propose to do?*
> *Go around here.*
> *What do you propose to make this movement with?*
> *With my whole corps.*
> *What will you leave me?*
> *The divisions of [Richard H.] Anderson and [Lafayette] McLaws.*

Jackson was proposing to leave Lee with 15,000 men to face 75,000 while he marched off into the Wilderness to find and attack the Union right flank. Lee calmly told him, "Well, go on." Of Jackson, he said:

> *I have but to show him my design, and I know that if it can be done, it will be done. No need for me to . . . watch him. Straight as the needle to the pole he advanced to the execution of my purpose.*

ADVICE

The perfect combination is the chief executive officer who can formulate bold strategic plans and the chief operating officer who can not only flawlessly implement them but will also take advantage of any opportunity to expand and enhance them. Such partnerships are rare. They can be developed through an association marked with complete openness and mutual trust and respect.

197. FIRST IMPRESSIONS

At THE START OF THE CAMPAIGN, HOOKER HAD announced, "My plans are perfect, and when I start to carry them out, may God have mercy on Bobby Lee, for I shall have none."

On the morning of May 2nd, Jackson's column was spotted, and Hooker informed the commander on his far right, General Oliver O. Howard, "We have good reason to suppose that the enemy is moving to our right." Hooker initially correctly surmised that Lee was trying to outflank him. He said, "It can't be a retreat. That is not Lee, to retreat without a fight."

On reflection, he concluded that his plan to crush Lee's army in a giant pincer was working perfectly. He convinced himself that Lee was not trying to outflank him. Hooker now believed that Lee had ordered a retreat when he realized he was going to be enveloped. Throughout the day, as reports of Jackson's column continued to come to his headquarters, Hooker persisted in his belief that Lee was retreating. Even the warning of a Confederate prisoner ("wait till Jackson gets around on your flank") went unheeded. At 4:30 p.m., Hooker sent the message, "We know the enemy is fleeing." Half an hour later, Jackson struck. His attack rolled up the Union right flank and created such panic that only nightfall prevented a rout.

ADVICE

First impressions are often the best. However, if your opinion, no matter when arrived at or how strongly held, is not supported by the facts, you need to change your opinion. Don't make the mistake of reinterpreting the facts to fit your preconceived notion.

Howard, who lost his right arm in the war, founded Howard University in Washington, D. C. and Lincoln Memorial University in Harrogate, Tennessee.

$\mathcal{W}$HILE RETURNING TO HIS OWN LINES AFTER reconnoitering the enemy positions in preparation for launching a night attack, General Jackson and his party were fired upon by Confederate pickets who mistook them for Union cavalry. Jackson was wounded, and the surgeons were forced to amputate his left arm.

Jeb Stuart assumed command of Jackson's corps. He sent a message to Jackson requesting instructions, but the wounded Jackson could only reply, "Say to General Stuart he must do what he thinks best." Not knowing Jackson was planning a night attack that would cut off the Union line of retreat and lead to the capture or destruction of Hooker's army, Stuart waited until morning to renew the assault. The next day the Confederates drove the Union troops from their positions at Chancellorsville, but they failed to win a decisive victory.

After the battle, Lee sent Jackson the following message:

Could I have directed events, I would have chosen for the good of the country to be disabled in your stead.

I congratulate you upon the victory, which is due to your skill and energy.

While recuperating, Jackson contracted pneumonia. He died on May 10, 1863. The day after he died, Lee wrote to his son, Custis, "It is a terrible loss. I do not know how to replace him."

ADVICE

There is no such thing as an irreplaceable person, but in the short term, the sudden and unexpected loss of a key player can be a devastating blow. To mitigate the effects of such a loss make sure that your subordinates and theirs are kept up-to-date on current operations and future plans.

$\mathcal{G}$ENERAL JUBAL EARLY WAS COMMANDING THE 10,000-man force that Lee had left at Fredericksburg. In his report on the battle of Chancellorsville, Lee wrote:

> *General Early had been instructed, in the event of the enemy withdrawing from his front . . . to join the main body of the army. . . . This order was repeated on the 2nd [of May], but by a misapprehension on the part of the officer conveying it, General Early was directed to move unconditionally.*

Lee had told a staff officer what to tell Early, but the officer delivered an incorrect message. As a result, Union troops were able to occupy Fredericksburg and threaten the rear of Lee's army. Lee was forced to postpone an attack against the main body of Hooker's army for two days, until he could drive off the Union troops who were marching on him from Fredericksburg. By the morning of May 6, 1863, when Lee was again ready to attack, Hooker had made good his escape by re-crossing the Rappahannock.

A D V I C E

Important instructions, even simple ones, need to be communicated in writing or face-to-face. Entrusting their transmission through a third party is a surefire recipe for disaster.

*I*N SPITE OF LEE'S VICTORY AT CHANCELLORSVILLE, THE overall war picture did not look good. Union General Ulysses S. Grant was closing in on Vicksburg, the Confederate bastion on the Mississippi River. If Vicksburg fell, the Confederacy would be split in two. When it was suggested that Lee send part of his army west to relieve the pressure on Vicksburg, he questioned the effectiveness of such a move.

Lee believed "the readiest method of relieving the pressure" in the West would be for his army to invade the North. Lee wanted to gain a decisive victory. He hoped that the destruction of the Army of the Potomac would so strengthen the hand of those in the North who favored peace that it would lead to an early end of the war. He was concerned that, if the war dragged on, the South would be overwhelmed by the seemingly inexhaustible resources of the North. As he explained to President Davis:

> *While making the most of the means of resistance we possess, and gratefully accepting the measure of success with which God has blessed our efforts. . . . We should not . . . conceal from ourselves that our resources in men are constantly diminishing, and the disproportion in this respect between us and our enemies . . . is steadily augmenting.*

Davis vacillated between following a defensive strategy of garrisoning important points and holding on until the North lost the will to fight, and "the best defense is a good offense" strategy that Lee wished to follow. In the end, perhaps without even realizing it, he tried to pursue both strategies simultaneously. He approved Lee's plan for a second invasion of the North, but he withheld from the invasion force five of Lee's brigades. These were composed of experienced soldiers and commanded by competent officers. Their presence at Gettysburg might have enabled Lee to win the victory the Confederacy so desperately needed.

A D V I C E

It's a mistake to pursue two conflicting strategies simultaneously, but that doesn't prevent some organizations from doing just that. The key to preventing this from happening is to recognize when the strategies are in conflict. One obvious warning sign is a situation that requires you to "rob from Peter to pay Paul" in order to pursue both paths simultaneously.

201. THE RIGHT PEOPLE

*D*AVIS DID AUGMENT LEE'S ARMY WITH TWO BRIGADES, but these were filled with green troops and commanded by inexperienced officers. Lee knew that filling his ranks with inexperienced men would hurt rather than help him. In reply to a general who had recommended an exchange of brigades, Lee wrote:

> *The plan you propose . . . I fear will add but little to its [my army's] real strength. It would increase it numerically but weaken it intrinsically by taking away tried troops under experienced officers and replacing them with fresh men and uninstructed commanders. I should therefore have more to feed but less to depend on.*

ADVICE

Lee wrote that his "army would be invincible if it could be properly organized and officered." Throwing people at a problem won't solve it unless they are properly trained and led by competent and experienced managers.

202. INCOMPETENCE OR INSUBORDINATION

$\mathcal{O}$N MAY 11, 1863, LEE TOLD PRESIDENT DAVIS THAT HE was going to "place General D. H. Hill in command of the department between James River and Cape Fear." On May 30th, Lee wrote to Davis:

> I gave General D. H. Hill discretionary instructions . . . to apportion his force to the strength of the enemy, and send me every man he could spare. He declined to act under those instructions, and requested positive instructions. He now offers objections. . . . You will see that I am unable to operate under these circumstances, and request to be relieved from any control of the department from the James to Cape Fear. . . . I have directed him [General Hill] to suspend the execution of the orders from me, and await orders from the Adjutant and Inspector General.

Instead of asking to be relieved of the responsibility for Hill's department, Lee should have relieved Hill, and instead of honoring Lee's request, Davis should have advised Lee to fire Hill.

ADVICE

Sun Tzu taught that, if you explain what you want and your subordinate fails to carry out your orders, it could be because you didn't make yourself clear. If you again explain what you want and your subordinate again fails to carry out your orders, it is because your subordinate is either incompetent or insubordinate. In either case, the proper remedy is for you to tell him or her to find another job.

203. QUALITY, NOT QUANTITY

*O*N JUNE 8, 1863, LEE REVIEWED JEB STUART'S CAVALRY. Later that day, he wrote to the Chief of Ordnance, Colonel Josiah Gorgas, to inform him that the cavalrymen were complaining about the saddles and carbines manufactured in Richmond:

> *I . . . was assured by officers that the former ruined the horses' backs, and the latter were so defective as to be demoralizing to the men. I am aware of the difficulties attending the manufacture of arms and equipment. . . . It would be better I think to make fewer articles and have them serviceable.*

ADVICE

Make sure your purchasing department understands that quality is your first consideration. Once baselines have been established for the quality of the equipment your people need, then other factors, such as cost and delivery schedules, can be used to differentiate among the suppliers who can meet your quality standards.

204. INFLEXIBLE POSITIONS

$\mathcal{O}$N JUNE 10TH, LEE SUGGESTED TO JEFFERSON DAVIS that the Confederacy attempt to encourage those in the North who favored opening peace negotiations. Concerned that adamant expressions by Confederate leaders that the Southern states would never return to the Union were making it impossible to advance the peace process, Lee wrote:

> *Should the belief that peace will bring back the Union become general, the war would no longer be supported [in the North], and that after all is what we are interested in bringing about. When peace is proposed to us it will be time enough to discuss its terms, and it is not the [better] part of prudence to spurn the proposition in advance, merely because those who wish to make it believe . . . that it will result in bringing us back to the Union.*

ADVICE

Most issues are resolved through compromise. Taking an inflexible position is like wearing cement overshoes. You lack the mobility needed to reach agreement.

205. YESTERDAY'S SUCCESS, TODAY'S FAILURE

As THE ARMY OF NORTHERN VIRGINIA MOVED NORTH, Lee gave his cavalry commander, Jeb Stuart, orders to "take a position on General [Richard S.] Ewell's right, place yourself in communication with him . . . keep him informed of the enemy's movements."

Stuart had made a name for himself by riding around McClellan's army before the start of the Seven Days' battles. During that ride, he had been unable to maintain communication with Lee. Then both armies were stationary, and Lee knew where the enemy was. Stuart decided to repeat his feat of riding around the Union army, but this time the circumstances were different. Both armies were in motion, and Lee did not know where the enemy was.

As his army marched north, Lee told one of his generals, "I cannot think what has become of Stuart. I ought to have heard from him long before now. . . . In the absence of reports from him, I am in ignorance as to what we have in front of us." On the morning of July 1st, Confederate and Union forces collided by accident at Gettysburg, Pennsylvania. Stuart did not show up until the following afternoon. When Lee saw him, he said, "General Stuart, where have you been? I have not heard from you in days, and you the eyes and ears of my army."

ADVICE

Trying to blindly emulate a past success will usually lead to failure, since the circumstances which enabled you to achieve that success are almost certain to have changed.

206. NEW BALL GAME

*W*HEN LEE LEARNED THAT THE NEW COMMANDER OF the Union Army of the Potomac was General George G. Meade, he told his staff:

General Meade will commit no blunder in my front, and if I make one he will make haste to take advantage of it.

ADVICE

When a competitor puts a new person in charge, particularly if his or her predecessor was replaced due to poor performance, you need to recognize that it could be the start of a new ball game, and act accordingly.

Lee and Meade had served together in Mexico. When they met at Appomattox after Lee surrendered, Lee said, "Meade, years are telling on you. Your hair is getting quite gray." Meade replied, "Ah, General Lee, it is not the work of years. You are responsible for my gray hairs."

207. LEARNING CURVE

*T*HE NEW COMMANDER OF JACKSON'S OLD CORPS WAS General Richard Ewell. Late in the afternoon of the first day at Gettysburg (July 1, 1863), Lee saw an opportunity for Ewell to occupy Cemetery Hill. As Walter Taylor recalled:

[General Lee] directed me to go to General Ewell and say to him that, from the position which he occupied, he could see the enemy retreating over those hills, without organization and in great confusion; that it was only necessary to press "those people" in order to secure possession of the heights, and that, if possible, he wished him to do this.

Ewell decided to wait until another of his divisions had come up before continuing the pursuit, even though a general who was with him offered to take Cemetery Hill if Ewell would let him have a division or a brigade or just a "good regiment." By the time Ewell was ready to move, darkness had fallen and the Union had occupied the high ground in force.

Lee believed that Jackson would have taken and held the heights that Ewell failed to secure. Then the Confederates would have held the high ground. He told a friend, "If I had had Stonewall Jackson with me . . . I should have won the battle of Gettysburg."

A D V I C E

Newly promoted people have a learning curve. The newer they are to the organization the longer the curve. Until you are comfortable that they are fully proficient in their new jobs, limit your discretionary instructions. Give direct and unambiguous orders, and maintain close contact so that you can help them deal with any difficulties they encounter.

Ewell had served under Jackson, and so was not new to the army or the corps he now commanded, but he had lost a leg in battle and only returned to active duty in May 1863, after a nine-month absence.

208. STAY ON THEIR CASE

$\mathcal{L}$EE ORDERED AN ATTACK FOR THE MORNING OF July 2nd. The main assault would be directed by Longstreet against the Union positions on Lee's right. Longstreet was opposed to Lee's plan and argued strenuously for his own alternative, a flanking movement to be followed by taking up defensive positions in anticipation of an enemy attack. This Lee rejected as being impractical. As Longstreet recalled:

I saw he was in no frame of mind to listen to further argument at that time, so I did not push the matter, but determined to renew the subject the next morning.

Before going to bed, Lee told his staff, "Gentlemen, we will attack the enemy as early in the morning as practicable." The next morning, Longstreet again tried to make a case for a flanking movement, and Lee again repeated his orders to attack. Lee then left Longstreet to confer with Ewell. About 10:00 a.m. he remarked, "What can detain Longstreet? He ought to be in position by now." Lee met with Longstreet about an hour later and again ordered him to attack.

Lee had remarked to one of his sons that Longstreet was "so slow" that he needed to stay close to him "in order to hasten his movements." Yet, during the remainder of the day, as Lee watched and waited, he sent Longstreet only one message, and he received only one from him. It was 4:00 p.m. before Longstreet attacked, and the attack was unsuccessful. Lee would later tell a friend, "The battle would have been gained if General Longstreet had obeyed the order given to him and attacked early instead of late."

ADVICE

When you have subordinates that are slow to act, especially when you know they have reservations about carrying out your instructions, you need to stay beside them until you are satisfied that they are doing all they can to successfully carry out your plans. If you sense that a subordinate's reservations are so strong that he or she will only give you half-hearted support, you should give the assignment to someone else.

209. IT'S STILL YOUR FIGHT

As Longstreet's troops advanced late on the afternoon of July 2nd, General John B. Hood requested permission to alter the plan of attack and outflank the Union defenders on Round Top. Longstreet replied, "General Lee's orders are to attack up the Emmitsburg Road." Twice more Hood asked for permission to flank Round Top. Longstreet answered, "We must obey the orders of General Lee." He failed to exercise the discretion that Lee granted his senior officers, and he refused to refer the matter to Lee. He wrote that "to delay and send messengers . . . would have been contumacious."

The following day Longstreet was ordered to attack the center of the Union line. Longstreet told Lee:

I have been a soldier all my life. . . . It is my opinion that no fifteen thousand men ever arrayed for battle can take that position.

Longstreet's adjutant remembered that at Gettysburg, "There was apparent apathy in his [Longstreet's] movements. They lacked the fire and point of his usual bearing on the battlefield." As General George E. Pickett's men advanced, Longstreet learned that the artillery was nearly out of ammunition. He wanted to stop Pickett until the ammunition could be replenished, but on learning that that would take too long, he said:

I don't want to make this charge. I don't believe it can succeed. I would stop Pickett, but that General Lee has ordered it and expects it.

Once again Longstreet failed to exercise discretion, and he failed to tell Lee that he didn't have enough ammunition to properly support the assault. Of this, the final day at Gettysburg, Longstreet wrote:

He [Lee] knew that I did not believe that success was possible . . . and he should have put an officer in charge who had more confidence in his plan.

ADVICE

If you don't believe a plan will work, you have an obligation to say so. If, after you've been heard, your boss sticks with his or her original plan, you have only two options: you can ask that the assignment be given to someone else, or you can attempt to carry it out to the best of your ability. Voicing your objections does not relieve you of responsibility for the outcome.

210. FALSE IMPRESSIONS

AFTER THE WAR, LONGSTREET WROTE THAT WHEN THE idea to invade Pennsylvania was first discussed he had asked Lee to make "the policy of the campaign one of defensive tactics. . . . To this he readily assented as an important and material adjunct to his general plan." Another victory like Fredericksburg was what Longstreet had in mind. While Lee would have been delighted to fight a defensive battle, he wanted to win a decisive victory, and he realized in order to do that he probably would have to be the attacker. On the march into Pennsylvania, Lee told one of his generals that he expected the Union army to be "broken down with hunger and hard marching, strung out on a long line and much demoralized, when they come into Pennsylvania."

I shall throw an overwhelming force on their advance, crush it, follow up the success, drive one corps back on another, and by successive repulses and surprises . . . create a panic and virtually destroy the army.

Longstreet believed that Lee, by attacking at Gettysburg, had gone back on his promise to fight a defensive battle. Lee was surprised to learn this. A friend remembered that Lee told him, "He had never made any such promise, and had never thought of doing any such thing." When Longstreet first brought up the subject of a defensive campaign, Lee, in his invariably gracious manner, probably so politely brushed the suggestion aside that Longstreet didn't realize that Lee had not agreed to his proposal. In turn, this likely soured Longstreet's attitude and impacted his performance during the campaign.

A D V I C E

Always state your position clearly. If you tell one of your
subordinates "no," don't leave him or her with the impression that what you meant was "maybe." You want to be
polite and try not to hurt people's feelings, but be careful
not to give the wrong impression and create misunderstandings.

After Lee died, the following note that he had written was found among his
papers: "Truth . . . will carry you through this world much better than policy, or
tact, or expediency, or any other word that was ever devised to conceal or mystify
a deviation from a straight line."

211. IN THE WAKE OF A DISASTER, I

As the survivors of "Pickett's Charge" fell back to the Confederate lines, Lee was concerned that Meade would counterattack. Circulating among the returning men, he spoke words intended to cheer, reassure and rally them: "All this will come right in the end. We'll talk it over afterwards, but, in the meantime, all good men must rally." Those who were only slightly wounded, he told to take up their muskets. To a general, who was very agitated, he said:

Never mind, General, all this has been my fault. It is I who have lost this fight, and you must help me out of it in the best way you can.

Stuart, Ewell and Longstreet all bore a share of the responsibility for the defeat at Gettysburg. Lee didn't look to apportion blame. He had been in charge. If the Confederates had won, it would have been his victory. Now, it was his defeat. Admitting he had made a mistake and taking full responsibility for it helped to keep the army's morale intact. One soldier expressed the army's feelings best when he told a British observer:

We've not lost confidence in the old man. This day's work will do him no harm. Uncle Robert will get us into Washington yet. You bet he will.

ADVICE

The first thing to do in the wake of a disaster is fix the problem. This is not the time for soul-searching or laying blame. Good leaders know that taking the responsibility on their own shoulders is the first step to getting the organization back on its feet in the shortest possible time.

212. IN THE WAKE OF A DISASTER, II

*O*N JUNE 25TH, A WEEK BEFORE THE START OF THE BATTLE of Gettysburg, Lee had expressed to Jefferson Davis his belief that he would be able to draw the Union army out of northern Virginia, "embarrassing their plan of campaign . . . if I can do nothing more and have to return." He had done that, but the South had paid dearly for that limited respite. When the casualty lists were compiled, it was clear that Gettysburg had been a horrendous battle. Over 50,000 Confederate and Union soldiers were dead, wounded or missing. Lee's casualties totaled one-third of his army. After Lee brought what remained of his army safely back to Virginia, he wrote to Davis:

> *The general remedy for the want of success in a military commander is his removal. This is natural, and in many instances proper. For no matter what may be the ability of the officer, if he loses the confidence of his troops disaster must sooner or later ensue.*
>
> *I have been prompted by these reflections more than once since my return from Pennsylvania to propose to Your Excellency the propriety of selecting another commander for this army. I have seen and heard of expressions of discontent in the public journals at the result of the expedition. I do not know how far this feeling extends in the army. . . . It is fair, however, to suppose that it does exist, and success is so necessary to us that nothing should be risked to secure it. I therefore, in all sincerity, request Your Excellency to take measures to supply my place.*

ADVICE

Good leaders admit when they've made a mistake. They take full responsibility for that mistake, and they accept the consequences for their actions.

Davis told Lee, "Misfortune often develops secret foes and oftener makes men complain. It is comfortable to hold someone responsible for one's discontent. . . . If a victim would secure the success of the cause, I would freely offer myself." He refused to accept Lee's resignation.

213. POSTMORTEMS

$\mathcal{T}$WO OF LEE'S STAFF OFFICERS REMEMBERED THAT, THE night before Pickett's charge, they had heard Lee order Longstreet to support the attack with his other divisions. After the attack failed, Lee told one of his officers that if Pickett's men "had been supported as they were to have been—but for some reason not yet fully explained to me, were not . . . the day would have been ours." Pickett, in his report of the battle, was critical of his superiors for failing to support the attack. When Lee received Pickett's report, he replied:

You and your men have crowned yourselves with glory, but we have the enemy to fight, and must carefully, at this critical moment, guard against dissensions which the reflections in your report would create. I will, therefore, suggest that you destroy both copy and original, substituting one confined to casualties merely.

A D V I C E

There is a big difference between the airing of grievances that tears an organization apart internally and damages its public image, and burying the bodies so quickly that no lessons are learned from the bad experience. Properly conducted postmortems reveal the reasons for the disaster and provide recommendations for avoiding future ones. If the failure is a public one, releasing a summary of the recommendations may help to reestablish confidence in the management of the organization.

After Gettysburg, Lee wrote, "We must expect reverses, even defeats. They are sent to teach us wisdom and prudence . . . and to prevent our falling into greater disasters."

*B*EFORE SETTING OUT ON THE CAMPAIGN, LEE HAD explained to Jefferson Davis that if the entire Union Army of the Potomac concentrated upon his smaller Army of Northern Virginia "it will result in our accomplishing nothing, and being compelled to return to Virginia." To help even the odds that he would be facing, Lee suggested putting some of the Confederacy's underutilized troops to better use.

I can see no benefit to be derived from maintaining a large force on the southern coast during the unhealthy months of summer and autumn, and I think that a part at least, of the troops in North Carolina, and of those under General Beauregard [in South Carolina], can be employed at this time with great advantage in Virginia. If an army could be organized under the command of General Beauregard, and pushed forward to Culpeper Court House, threatening Washington from that direction. . . . The well known anxiety of the Northern Government for the safety of its capital would induce it to retain a large force for its defense, and thus sensibly relieve the opposition to our advance. . . . If success should attend the operations of this army, and what I now suggest would greatly increase the probability of that result, we might even hope to compel the recall of some of the enemy's troops from the west.

Davis did not act on Lee's suggestion, and, at Gettysburg, the Confederates had once again been outnumbered.

A D V I C E

Use the plan review process to make certain that your organization is applying all its available resources toward accomplishing your goals. Leave no hands idle in achieving your purpose.

215. SOLE SOURCES OF SUPPLY

*T*HE CONFEDERATE CAPITAL, RICHMOND, HAD BECOME a major center for the production of war materials. Lee was troubled by the concentration of manufacturing plants in Richmond, since the capture or destruction of the city was a prime objective of the Union war effort. In September 1863, Lee sent President Davis the following suggestion:

Colonel [Josiah] Gorgas should commence at once to enlarge his manufacturing arsenals, etc., in the interior, so that if Richmond should fall we would not be destitute. These are only recommended as prudential measures, and such as should be necessary for them to arise, we will then wish had been taken.

A D V I C E

It is foolish to be dependent upon a single source of supply. If your business is large enough, you may be able to encourage the development of alternative suppliers. If that is impractical, you should look to diversify, so as to minimize the disruption that would occur in the event your sole source of supply was interrupted.

 FTER DEFEATING LEE AT GETTYSBURG, MEADE followed him back to Northern Virginia. There, in the fall of 1863, Meade had two small additional successes, Bristoe Station (October 14th) where A. P. Hill ran into an ambush, and Kelly's Ford (November 7th) where an advance guard was caught flatfooted by a night attack.

When Meade advanced in late November, Lee, though greatly outnumbered, saw his chance to attack at Mine Run. On the morning of December 2nd, the Confederates advanced only to discover that the Union army had once again retreated. The campaign for the year was over, and both armies went into winter quarters. When Lee learned that Meade had escaped, he said:

I am too old to command this army. We should never have permitted those people to get away.

When Lee made that remark he was one month shy of his 57th birthday. In March 1863, Lee had told his wife, "Old age and sorrow is wearing me away, and constant anxiety and labor, day and night, leaves me but little repose." Later that month, he had what doctors now believe was a heart attack, from which he never fully recovered. In the letter of resignation he had written after the battle of Gettysburg, Lee had given his health as a reason for wanting to step down: "I sensibly feel the growing failure of my bodily strength. I have not yet recovered from the attack I experienced the past spring."

ADVICE

There comes a time when you won't feel as sharp or as engaged as you once were. When your strength starts to fail or your attention starts to wane, you need to begin thinking about doing something else. If you no longer have the energy or you've lost the hunger for the job, go gracefully without waiting to be told.

In refusing to accept Lee's resignation, Davis had explained, "To ask me to substitute [for] you . . . some one in my judgment more fit to command, or who would possess more of the confidence of the army, or of the reflecting men of the country, is to demand an impossibility."

217. INTERIM SOLUTIONS

*I*N LATE NOVEMBER 1863, ULYSSES S. GRANT DEFEATED the Confederate forces at Chattanooga, Tennessee. Davis asked Lee if he could assume temporary command of the army that Grant had just driven into northern Georgia. On December 7th, Lee replied:

I can if desired, but of the expediency of the measure you can judge better than I can. Unless it is intended that I should take permanent command, I can see no good that will result.

ADVICE

Try to avoid interim solutions, especially when they involve putting someone in charge temporarily. It is difficult enough for a new manager to gain the support that he or she will need to be successful. Once people in the organization realize the new manager is temporary, he or she doesn't stand a chance. Also, interim managers are always looking ahead to their next permanent assignment. They may feel the need to get results quickly so as to be able to earn a choice permanent post. Knowing that they won't be around to deal with the long-term consequences of the actions they take to achieve those results, they may be tempted to try quick fixes that cover up but do not cure the problem.

218. DUMB REGULATIONS

*I*N FEBRUARY 1864, LEE WROTE TO THE SECRETARY OF War to object to his interpretation of the law regarding promotions:

> *The present position of the Department . . . seems to be that an officer or private can only be promoted for valor and skill to a vacancy in his own company. This limits the promotions for valor and skill to such an extent that it renders the law almost a dead letter. . . . It is very important to increase the numbers of these promotions.*

A D V I C E

What you don't need are dumb regulations. Bureaucrats have an uncanny ability to promulgate rules that are counterproductive. All proposed rules and regulations should be reviewed and approved by the managers who will have to live with them. Periodically, all of your organization's rules and regulations should be reviewed to see if any need to be revised or discarded.

Lee said, "Make no needless rules."

219. HELP THEM GET IN THE GAME

*L*EE'S ELDEST SON, CUSTIS, HAD GRADUATED FIRST IN his class at West Point and had been in the Corps of Engineers prior to the start of the Civil War. He was serving on the staff of President Davis when he was offered the opportunity for a field command. Custis had never commanded troops, and he was hesitant to accept the assignment. On March 29, 1864, Lee offered him this counsel:

> *No one can predict with certainty with what success you would operate, but I think you will do as well as those . . . who have preceded you. I see no reason why you should not be successful. . . . The time is coming, indeed has come, when everyone . . . must take those positions where it is reasonably evident they will be of most value. . . . You refuse command because you have no experience in the field. I appreciate the motives. But until you come in the field you never will gain experience.*

ADVICE

For some, taking that first management job can be a frightening experience. You need to reassure them that all they lack is experience, and the only way to get it is to come off the sidelines and get in the game.

Custis did accept a field command later that year. He was captured at the battle of Sayler's Creek, fought three days before Lee surrendered at Appomattox.

$\mathcal{U}$NLIKE SOME GENERALS, LEE DIDN'T BELIEVE IN sending a flurry of messages to all the men in the army. He issued general orders only when the occasion demanded it. On the march into Pennsylvania, he had reminded his men of how he expected them to conduct themselves:

> *The commanding general considers that no greater disgrace could befall the army . . . than the perpetration of the barbarous outrages . . . and the wanton destruction of private property that have marked the course of the enemy in our own country.*

> *Such proceedings . . . are subversive of the discipline and efficiency of the army, and destructive of the ends of our present movement.*

> *It must be remembered that we make war only upon armed men, and that we cannot take vengeance for the wrongs our people have suffered without . . . offending against Him to whom vengeance belongeth, without whose favor and support our efforts must all prove in vain.*

In April 1864, as his army prepared for the upcoming campaign, Lee told his men what he expected of them should they become prisoners of war:

> *We cannot spare brave men to fill Federal prisons. Should, however, any be so unfortunate as to fall through unavoidable necessity into the hands of the enemy, it is important that they should preserve entire silence with regard to everything connected to the army. . . . Proper prudence on the part of all will be of great assistance in preserving that secrecy so essential to success.*

ADVICE

Some senior executives pester their people with a seemingly endless stream of memos. Their people quickly become amused and then bored by this unnecessary attention. The memos usually hit the trash bin unread. Save your "all employee" memos for when you have something important to say.

THE WINNING
IMAGE

May 1864–April 1865

For eleven months, Lee holds at bay the overwhelming forces commanded by Ulysses S. Grant. He stymies the Union commander in the Wilderness, at Spotsylvania Court House, on the North Anna River, at Cold Harbor, and during the siege of Petersburg. But even he cannot prevent the collapse of the Confederacy. On April 9, 1865, he surrenders the Army of Northern Virginia. Instead of feeling elated by his victory, General Grant feels "sad and depressed at the downfall of a foe who had fought so long and valiantly." When his troops begin to celebrate, he tells them to stop because "the rebels are our countrymen again." At the formal surrender ceremony, the Union army salutes as the Confederates march by. Lee tells his men:

I have done the best I could for you. Go home now, and if you make as good citizens as you have soldiers, you will do well, and I shall always be proud of you. Goodbye, and God bless you all.

221. SMOOTHING RUFFLED FEATHERS

*L*EE ALWAYS SEEMED TO BE ABLE TO TELL WHEN someone headed his way was angry. He would step into his tent and, closing the flap behind him, call out to Walter Taylor, "Assuage him, Colonel, 'suage him, and send him away." Lee would let his staff deal with minor issues, but the serious ones he dealt with himself. To a general who had requested a transfer, Lee wrote:

I require your services here. You must come and see me and tell me what is the matter. I know you are too good a soldier not to serve where it is necessary for the benefit of the Confederacy.

ADVICE

People occasionally need to vent, but harsh words spoken about trivial matters can result in damaged relations. Having them express their frustrations to a secretary or administrative aide can prevent a needless confrontation. Serious matters are another story. They require your personal attention.

222. ANGER IS CONTAGIOUS

$\mathcal{W}$ALTER TAYLOR WROTE THAT LEE "WAS NOT ONE OF those invariably amiable men whose temper is never ruffled."

On one occasion. . . . He was not in a very pleasant mood...and he manifested his ill humor by a little nervous twist or jerk of the neck and head . . . accompanied by some harshness of manner. . . . I hastily concluded that my efforts to save him annoyance were not appreciated. In disposing of some case . . . I petulantly threw the paper down at my side and gave evident signs of anger. Then, in a perfectly calm and measured tone of voice, he said, "Colonel Taylor, when I lose my temper, don't you let it make you angry."

ADVICE

Anger is contagious and counterproductive. Don't exhibit anger, and don't let someone else's anger cause you to lose your temper. When dealing with an angry person, calmly acknowledge the anger and then move on to a discussion of causes and remedies.

223. SELF-CONTROL

*W*HILE LEE DID OCCASIONALLY LOSE HIS TEMPER, Walter Taylor admired "his remarkable self-control."

When we consider the immense burden which rested upon him, and the numberless causes for annoyance with which he had to contend, the occasional cropping out of temper which we, who were constantly near him, witnessed, only showed how great was his habitual self-command.

ADVICE

It's a mistake to retain in management people who lack self-control. When you are faced with a situation involving someone who can't keep his or her temper in check, remember Lee's perspective, "I cannot consent to place in the control of others one who cannot control himself."

While Lee's comment was in reference to a man who drank too much, it is equally applicable to someone who fails to control his or her temper.

224. RESPECT AND CONSIDERATION

$\mathcal{O}$NE DAY, LEE SAW A SOLDIER NEAR HIS TENT. HE SAID to the man:

Come in, Captain, and take a seat.

I'm no captain, General. I'm nothing but a private.

Come in, sir. Come in and take a seat. You ought to be a captain.

One Confederate officer wrote that Lee's "theory, expressed upon many occasions, was that the private soldiers . . . were the most meritorious class of the army, and that they deserved and should receive the utmost respect and consideration."

A D V I C E

Good leaders never forget that they rise to success on the shoulders of their people.

225. DON'T TAKE THEM FOR GRANTED

*W*ALTER TAYLOR STARTED WORKING FOR LEE IN MAY 1861, and served for the duration of the war. They saw each other almost every day. No one worked more closely with Lee than Taylor. That Lee thought highly of Taylor is clear from the recommendation he wrote in support of Taylor's promotion to lieutenant colonel:

He is intelligent, industrious, and acquainted in the discharge of his duties, and his character irreproachable—I know of no better person for the appointment.

Lee, who was so careful to praise the deserving officers and men of his army, didn't always show the same consideration for the men on his personal staff. Taylor complained, "Everybody else makes me flattering speeches, but I want to satisfy him. They all say he appreciates my efforts, but I don't believe it."

ADVICE

Those you work with most closely can be like family to you. Unfortunately, all too frequently, people take their family for granted.

226. SOMEONE IS WATCHING

WHILE THE ARMY WAS IN WINTER QUARTERS, WIVES could visit their husbands. Some would stay at homes in the vicinity of the army's encampment. With the coming of spring and the start of another season of active campaigning, Lee would order the women to the rear. By chance, Lee met with a captain and his wife, who had not yet left, even though the order had been given some time ago. The woman immediately tried to apologize for not promptly obeying Lee's order, but Lee put her at ease.

My order was not intended for you at all. It was intended only for your husband. I intend to get a great deal of work out of him this summer, and he cannot do his work unless his horses are in condition. Every evening for some weeks, about nightfall, I have observed that he mounted his horse behind his camp and galloped off to Orange Courthouse, three miles away, and every morning he came galloping back about sunrise. Now you know this is not good for the horses. By the time I should need his services they would be worn out, and I was obliged to put a stop to it.

The captain remembered that "there was in General Lee's little joke a reproof and warning to me . . . he let me know that he had his eye on me, and that he knew more of my movements than had been supposed."

A D V I C E

Don't think you aren't being observed. You are.

227. INSPECTIONS

*W*HEN AN OFFICER ASKED LEE TO INSPECT HIS MEN, Lee replied:

Colonel, a dirty camp gives me nausea. If you say your camps are clean, I will go.

ADVICE

Scheduled visits to field locations can be as beneficial as unannounced ones. Let your people know in advance what you expect to see.

228. LOOK THROUGH THEIR EYES

*I*N MAY 1864, THE UNION ARMY OF THE POTOMAC crossed the Rapidan River under the personal supervision of the new commanding general of the United States, Ulysses S. Grant. Lee checked Grant's advance in the Wilderness. In the battle, the Union army suffered as many casualties as it had at Chancellorsville. The Army of the Potomac had retreated after that battle. This time, Lee was convinced, it would not retreat. Instead, Grant would continue to move south toward Richmond.

Lee told one of his generals, "Spotsylvania is now General Grant's best strategic point." Lee won the race to Spotsylvania Court House and blocked Grant's advance after more hard fighting. Grant disengaged from Lee and marched to the North Anna River, only to find Lee, once again, had gotten there ahead of him. The Confederates were in such a strong defensive position that Grant chose not to attack. He made another flanking movement, this time to Cold Harbor. When he got there, Lee was waiting for him.

ADVICE

Never make the mistake of assuming your competitors will do something dumb. Instead, assume they know your every weakness and will take the actions you least wish them to take, the ones calculated to cause you the most grief. If you want to stay ahead of your competitors, put yourself in their shoes. Determine the best steps they could take, the ones you would take if they hired you to manage their organization.

229. BENCH STRENGTH

*L*ONGSTREET AND TWO OTHER GENERALS HAD BEEN seriously wounded in the battle of the Wilderness. Three had been killed. A. P. Hill was ill, and Lee had reservations about his other corps commander, Richard Ewell. During the fighting at Spotsylvania Court House, Lee was frequently exposed to enemy fire. On May 12th, when Union troops overran the Confederate positions in the Mule Shoe (Bloody Angle), Lee started to lead a counterattack. General John B. Gordon described what happened next.

Lee looked a very god of war. . . . I called out, "General Lee, you shall not lead my men in a charge. . . . These men . . . have never failed you on any field. They will not fail you here. . . ."

I shouted to General Lee, "You must go to the rear!"

The echo, "General Lee to the rear, General Lee to the rear!" rolled back . . . from my men; and they gathered around him . . . ready to shove him by main force to the rear.

At the end of the day, one of Lee's generals was dead, another was dying, three had been badly wounded, and two had been captured. That night, Lee received more bad news. Jeb Stuart had been mortally wounded the previous day at the battle of Yellow Tavern.

ADVICE

Even if you know all the roles, you can't play all the parts yourself. Successful organizations have a strong bench. Focus on developing future first-string players for every position.

A. P. Hill resumed command of his corps when the army began its march to the North Anna River. Longstreet rejoined the army in October 1864, during the siege of Petersburg.

230. DISTRACTIONS

*T*HOSE AROUND LEE WERE ALWAYS AMAZED THAT he seemed oblivious to the dangers that he was frequently exposed to in battle. He was aware of the risks, but he didn't allow himself to be distracted by them.

> *Necessary noise never troubles me. In the midst of battle, for instance, with the roar of artillery or musketry around me . . . and amid all the noise and hub-bub of such an occasion, I could sit on my horse, attend to my duties and write a dispatch or other papers, undisturbed by what was going on.*

A D V I C E

In business, you aren't faced with life-threatening situations, but there are plenty of everyday distractions. You have to be able to put them aside and stay focused.

231. DON'T PASS THE BUCK

$\mathcal{O}$N MAY 30TH, LEE TELEGRAPHED THE PRESIDENT'S military advisor, General Braxton Bragg, that a corps from the army of Union General Benjamin F. Butler had been sent to reinforce Grant. Lee also telegraphed General Beauregard, who was commanding at Petersburg, twenty miles south of Richmond, and requested reinforcements. Beauregard, who had the authority to move troops to Lee, replied:

War Department must determine when and what troops to order from here. I send to General Bragg all information I obtain relative to movement of enemy's troops in front.

Lee telegraphed back:

If you cannot determine what troops you can spare, the Department cannot. The result of your delay will be disaster. Butler's troops will be with Grant tomorrow.

Lee also told President Davis:

General Beauregard says the department must determine what troops to send from him. He gives it all necessary information. The result of this delay will be disaster.

Reinforcements were dispatched to Lee that night. They arrived in time to assist in beating back the Union assault at Cold Harbor on June 3rd.

ADVICE

You know your circumstances best. Don't try to kick a decision upstairs that you have the authority to make. All that does is delay the process, and delay can be costly. When dealing with someone who regularly passes the buck to his or her boss, send copies of all your communications to that person's boss, both to make sure your position isn't being misinterpreted and to keep from losing time.

At Cold Harbor, the Confederate defenders inflicted over 7,000 casualties on their attackers, while they themselves suffered less than 1,500. One of Lee's aides wrote that it was "perhaps the easiest victory ever granted...by the folly of the Federal commanders."

*O*N JUNE 12, 1864, LEE RECOMMENDED THAT GENERAL Ewell be relieved of command of his corps. Lee had been concerned with Ewell's performance since Gettysburg. In a letter he wrote to Ewell back in January, Lee had tried to give Ewell a graceful way out.

I do not know how much ought to be attributed to long absence from the field, general debility, or the result of your injury, but I was in constant fear during the last campaign that you would sink under your duties or destroy yourself. . . . You now know from experience what you have to undergo, and can best judge of your ability to endure it; I fear we cannot anticipate less labor than formerly.

Ewell did not take the hint and retained command of his corps during the opening phases of the 1864 campaign. Lee believed that Ewell's vacillation during the battle of the Wilderness prevented him from crushing the Union army. Had Lee relieved Ewell in January, he would have had three months, while both armies were inactive, to break in a new corps commander.

A D V I C E

Don't ask your people to read your mind. When you've decided what needs to be done, tell them. If you pose questions, you could get the wrong answers.

Field Marshal Viscount Wolseley, who had been a British observer with Lee's army, believed that Lee was the greatest soldier of his age, but "like all the greatest of generals, he sometimes made mistakes. His nature shrank with such horror from the dread of wounding the feelings of others, that upon occasions he left men in positions of responsibility to which their abilities were not equal."

233. IF IT'S BROKE, FIX IT

$\mathcal{L}$EE TOLD JUBAL EARLY THAT IF THE CONFEDERATES were unable to destroy Grant's army, "it will become a siege, and then it will be a mere question of time." On June 18, 1864, Lee informed President Davis that "Grant's whole force has crossed to the south side of the James River. . . . I have ordered all the troops over towards Petersburg." The siege that Lee dreaded had begun.

Lee had severely punished the Union army in the Wilderness and at Spotsylvania Court House and Cold Harbor, but his own losses had been heavy. In a siege the Union had the advantage because, as Union General George G. Meade explained, "It is in our power more promptly to fill the gaps in men and material which this constant fighting produces." At the start of the campaign, Lee was outnumbered two to one. As the siege wore on, the disparity between the opposing forces increased. In August, Lee told the Secretary of War:

Our numbers are daily decreasing, and the time has arrived in my opinion when no man should be excused from the service, except for the purpose of doing work absolutely necessary for the support of the army. . . . Without some increase in our strength, I cannot see how we are to escape the natural military consequences of the enemy's numerical superiority.

The following month, he informed General Bragg that he had learned that there were 40,000 able-bodied men in Virginia alone who had been exempted from military service.

I recommended to the President to have an inspection

made of the conscription service with a view to obtain accurate information as to its working. To me it now seems a very imperfect system.

Lee believed that if people with "energy, intelligence and practical ability" focused on "putting men in the army" the ranks would be filled.

A D V I C E

When you have a problem, you need to fix it promptly. Letting it drag on only makes it harder, and in some cases even impossible, to solve later.

To solve his other perennial problem, securing rations for his army, Lee gave the Secretary of War this advice: "The proper remedy is increased effort, greater experience in business, and intelligent management."

WHILE LEE HAD BEEN PREVENTING GRANT FROM taking Richmond, his old friend, Joe Johnston, had been keeping Sherman out of Atlanta. Sherman was so frustrated by Johnston's effective defense that he complained, "The whole country is one vast fort."

Jefferson Davis was impatient. He wanted Johnston to attack Sherman and win a decisive victory. Johnston realized his forces were too weak, and that he would be the one defeated if he attacked. Davis decided that Johnston's actions were too timid to suit him, and he replaced Johnston with General Hood. When Lee learned what Davis was planning to do, he immediately sent Davis the following telegram:

Telegram of today received. I regret the fact stated. It is a bad time to replace the commander. . . . We may lose Atlanta and the army too.

Davis didn't heed Lee's advice. Hood lost Atlanta at the beginning of September 1864, and he lost his army in December of that year at the battle of Nashville. Lincoln, whose election prospects had looked dim while Grant and Sherman were both bogged down, received a major boost from the fall of Atlanta and was returned to the White House. Had the Confederates held Atlanta until after the election of 1864, Lincoln's opponent, General McClellan, would likely have won, and a war-weary North might have agreed to let the Confederate States have their independence.

A D V I C E

Even if you are an expert and are up-to-date, let your professionals do their job. Hold them accountable for their performance, but don't second-guess them.

Ulysses S. Grant sarcastically remarked that Jefferson Davis had on several occasions come "to the relief of the Union army by means of his superior military genius."

235. SARCASM

To one of his generals, Lee remarked:

I have sometimes to admonish . . . General Gordon against being too fast. I shall never have occasion to find that fault with you.

During the siege, he greeted an officer, who tended to stay in the city of Petersburg, well behind the front lines, with the question:

General, are you not afraid to trust yourself so far from the city, and come to where all this firing and danger is?

ADVICE

Don't be sarcastic. People can become so confused or offended by your manner, tone and language that they miss or discount your message.

Lee rarely used sarcasm. As he explained: "When a man makes a mistake, I call him to my tent, talk to him, and use the authority of my position to make him do the right thing the next time."

*L*EE WOULD SOMETIMES TELL A STORY TO MAKE A POINT. In response to a rumored enemy movement, Lee had sent Charles Marshall to the front with orders. When Marshall arrived, he discovered the rumor was not true, and so did not deliver Lee's order. At dinner that evening, Lee asked Marshall if he had known General David E. Twiggs. Lee then told his staff this story:

When he [Twiggs] went to Mexico he had a number of young officers connected with his staff who were . . . very zealous and desirous to do their duty thoroughly. Sometimes they undertook General Twiggs' orders, and would fail to do what he had told them to do, or would not do it as the general had ordered it to be done. If General Twiggs remarked upon such liberties being taken with his orders, these gentlemen were always ready to show that they were right and that General Twiggs was wrong. The general bore this . . . for some time, but one day a young officer . . . reported that when he had reached the place where the thing ordered by General Twiggs was to be done, he had found the circumstances so entirely different . . . that he thought that the general would not have given the order had he known the fact, and was proceeding to satisfy General Twiggs that what . . . [he] had done was the best under the circumstances. But General Twiggs interrupted him by saying, "Captain, I know that you can prove that you are right, and that my order was wrong; in fact, you gentlemen are always right, but for God's sake do wrong sometimes."

ADVICE

Telling stories can be a very effective way to get across a message. Most people enjoy hearing a good anecdote. Storytelling works best in a relaxed group setting where your people can hear the message without any one of them feeling singled out for criticism. Abraham Lincoln was a masterful storyteller: "They say I tell a great many stories. I reckon I do; but I have learned from long experience that plain people, take them as they run, are more easily influenced through the medium of a broad and humorous illustration than in any other way."

237. MEANINGLESS TITLES

*O*VER PRESIDENT DAVIS' OBJECTIONS, THE CONFEDERATE Congress created the position of commanding general of all the armies. Davis was pressured into appointing Lee to the post on February 1, 1865. While Lee now had the title, he did not have the authority to go with it. When it was suggested to Lee that he should reappoint General Johnston to command of the army facing Sherman, he replied:

I can only employ such troops and officers as may be placed at my disposal by the War Department. Those withheld or relieved from service are not at my disposal.

A D V I C E

You place people in impossible situations when you put them in a job, but don't let them execute the managerial authority normally associated with that job's level of responsibility.

At Lee's urging, Davis reluctantly re-appointed Johnston to command of the army opposing Sherman.

$\mathcal{L}$EE TOLD GENERAL JOHN GORDON:

It is enough to turn one's hair gray to spend one day in the Congress. The members are patriotic and earnest, but they will neither take the responsibility of action nor will they clothe me with the authority to act for them.

On February 16, 1865, the *Richmond Examiner,* referring to Lee's appointment as commanding general of the Confederate armies, commented:

This clothes him with great power, and loads him with heavy responsibility. If he is willing to wield that power and shoulder that responsibility, in the name of God, let him have them.

If the Confederate Congress wanted Lee to assume the role of commander-in-chief, then it should have restricted President Davis' authority. Instead, Congress tried an end run around Davis with the creation of the post of commanding general of the armies. The members of Congress had hoped that Davis would get the message that they wanted him to delegate the management of the war to Lee, but Davis wrote that he lacked the "will to delegate."

ADVICE

End runs don't work. If the chief executive officer isn't doing the job, the board of directors should find a replacement. Trying to delegate some of his or her duties to a subordinate only works if the CEO is willing to relinquish those duties.

239. SENSE OF HUMOR

$\mathcal{G}$RANT HAD BEGUN THE CAMPAIGN OF 1864 WITH A two-to-one numerical superiority. As the siege of Petersburg wore on, the disparity between the Union and Confederate forces grew even greater. By the end of February 1865, Sheridan had laid waste to the Shenandoah Valley, and Sherman had taken Atlanta, marched across Georgia, captured Savannah, and then moved north into the Carolinas. Lee was under incredible strain. On March 2nd, Grant sent an officer to Lee to arrange for a truce so that Grant could bury his dead between the lines. The officer then delivered a personal message from Grant: "Give General Lee my personal compliments, and say to him that I keep such close touch with him that I know what he eats for breakfast every morning." As Lee recalled:

I told that officer to tell General Grant that I thought there must be some mistake . . . for unless he had fallen from grace since I last saw him, he would not permit me to eat such a breakfast as mine without dividing his with me. I also requested that officer to present my compliments to General Grant, and say to him that I knew perhaps as much about his dinners as he knew about my breakfasts.

ADVICE

Even under the most trying circumstances, try to keep your sense of humor. Laughter helps relieve strain. It is good medicine for both you and your subordinates.

240. OUT TO LUNCH

AT PETERSBURG, GRANT CONTINUED TO EXTEND HIS lines. Lee had warned President Davis, "I do not see how in our present position he [Grant] can be prevented from enveloping Richmond." Lee's lines were being stretched to the breaking point. On March 31, 1865, General Pickett, supported by cavalry under the command of Lee's nephew, General Fitzhugh Lee, stymied an attempt to turn Lee's right flank. The following day the Confederates took up defensive positions at Five Forks. Feeling that the situation was well in hand, and no Union attack was imminent, the two generals accepted an invitation to a fish fry. While they were out to lunch, their troops were attacked and routed by General Sheridan.

ADVICE

Walter Taylor wrote that Lee was "never so uncomfortable as when comfortable." Some managers find it easier to be sharp and focused when dealing with difficult situations than when things are going well. Bad things can happen during quiet periods. You can never allow yourself to become so relaxed that you fail to notice the storm waiting to break.

ON APRIL 2ND, GRANT ORDERED AN ASSAULT ON LEE'S defenses. At the end of the day's fighting, Lee told one of his aides, "It has happened as I told them it would. . . . The line has been stretched until it has broken." Lee informed Jefferson Davis that to avoid being surrounded, he would have to evacuate Petersburg that night, which he did. Lee got his army safely away, but he lost the day's head start he had on Grant when he had to stop to forage for food for his men. The rations he had requested had not been sent. The trains had been used instead to transport Confederate government personnel and records from Richmond. In a letter to Davis describing his army's final hours, he wrote, "This delay was fatal."

On April 6th, the Union army caught up with Lee at Sayler's Creek. His demoralized and starving men were in no condition to put up much of a fight. When it was over, Lee said, "That half of our army is destroyed." The following day, Lee received a note from Grant, "The result of the last week must convince you of the hopelessness of further resistance." Grant ended his note by asking Lee to surrender his army. Lee responded:

Though not entertaining the opinion you express of the hopelessness of further resistance on the part of the Army of Northern Virginia, I reciprocate your desire to avoid useless effusion of blood and therefore before considering your proposition ask the terms you will offer on condition of its surrender.

The next day, Lee received Grant's answer:

In reply I would say that peace being my great desire, there is but one condition I would insist upon, namely: that the men and officers surrendered shall be disqualified from taking up arms again, against the Government of the United States.

A D V I C E

Face-to-face negotiations are more likely to be successful if both sides come to the table having already agreed in principle on how to resolve the fundamental differences. Try to avoid entering into face-to-face negotiations until both parties have the same general understanding of what the final agreement will look like. The more you can accomplish during pre-negotiations, the better the chances of reaching a satisfactory conclusion when you sit down at the table.

242. SQUEEZE OUT AN EXTRA CONCESSION

*L*EE AND GRANT MET TO DISCUSS TERMS FOR THE surrender of the Army of Northern Virginia at Appomattox Court House on April 9, 1865. Grant began the conversation by mentioning that they had met once before during the Mexican War. After some reminiscing, Lee turned to the subject at hand. Grant stated that the terms on which he would receive the surrender were "those stated substantially in my letter . . . that is, the officers and men surrendered to be paroled." At Lee's request, Grant then committed the terms to writing. After Lee read them over, he said, "This will have a very happy effect upon my army." Grant's aide, Horace Porter, recalled their conversation:

General Grant then said: "Unless you have some suggestions to make in regard to the form in which I have stated the terms, I will have a copy . . . made in ink, and sign it."

"There is one thing I should like to mention," Lee replied, after a short pause. "The cavalrymen and artillerists own their own horses in our army. . . . I should like to understand whether these men will be permitted to retain their horses."

"You will find that the terms as written do not allow this," Grant replied; "only the officers are permitted to take their private property."

Lee read over the second page . . . again, and then said: "No, I see the terms do not allow it; that is clear." His face showed plainly that he was quite anxious to have this concession made; and Grant said very promptly, and without giving Lee time to make a direct request:

"Well, the subject is quite new to me. . . . I will arrange it in this way: I will not change the terms as now written, but I will instruct the officers I shall appoint to receive the paroles to let all the men who claim to own a horse or mule take the animals home with them."

Lee . . . gave every evidence of his appreciation of this concession, and said: "This will have the best possible effect upon the men. It will be very gratifying, and will do much toward conciliating our people."

A D V I C E

If the other party is satisfied with the outcome of your negotiations, then you usually can obtain an additional concession, even one that might have been a deal-breaker had it been mentioned before an agreement was reached.

243. THE WINNING IMAGE

*A*SKED AFTER THE WAR WHAT HIS FIRST THOUGHTS were on meeting Lee, Grant recalled that his own boots were dirty and that Lee was immaculately dressed. That morning when one of his generals had remarked on his dress, Lee had told him, "I have probably to be General Grant's prisoner and thought I must make my best appearance." Lee was wearing a new uniform with a red silk sash, and he was wearing his finest dress sword. Inscribed on the blade in French were the words "Help yourself, and God will help you."

Union General Joshua L. Chamberlain remembered seeing Lee as he rode to meet Grant:

I turned about, and there behind me . . . appeared a commanding form, superbly mounted, richly accoutered, of imposing bearing, noble countenance, with expression of deep sadness overmastered by deeper strength. It is no other than Robert E. Lee! And seen by me for the first time. . . . I sat immovable, with certain awe and admiration."

The image that Americans have of the surrender scene at Appomattox Court House is striking. Anyone who didn't know better would think that Grant was surrendering to Lee, not the other way around. While Lee's appearance, bearing and manner contribute to that image, the most important factors are his record of accomplishment and the spirit with which he infused his army.

As Grant left the house where he and Lee had met, and saw Lee on his horse starting back toward his lines, Grant removed his hat, and all the other Union officers standing in the yard did the same. It was a fitting tribute.

Three days later, at the formal surrender ceremony, General Chamberlain gave the command for the Union troops to salute as the veterans of the Army of Northern Virginia marched past. In saluting their defeated foe, the men of the Army of the Potomac were giving expression to feelings that have held to this day: Robert E. Lee and his army had been overwhelmed, but they had not been conquered.

A D V I C E

Cultivate a winning image. Even in the most trying times, your appearance, bearing and manner can give you greater power than your circumstances would actually warrant. Remember your past accomplishments with pride and hold your head high. To be perceived as a winner, you must never look or act like a loser.

On the morning of April 14, 1865, Abraham Lincoln was shown a photograph of Robert E. Lee. After carefully studying the picture, Lincoln said, "It's a good face. I am glad the war is over."

244. WHEN IT'S OVER

$\mathcal{O}$N MARCH 9, 1865, ONE MONTH BEFORE HE
surrendered, Lee wrote to the Secretary of War that "the
legitimate consequences of . . . [the enemy's] superiority
have been postponed longer than we had reason to anticipate." Lee knew the war was lost. He had told a
Confederate Senator:

*If you think there is a chance for a peace that would
get us better terms than they will give after surrender, it is
your duty to make the effort now.*

Lee also discussed the war situation with Jefferson
Davis, who refused to accept the fact that defeat was
inevitable. After his meeting with Davis, Lee told one of his
officers that the President had "remarkable faith in the possibility of still winning our independence."

On April 9th, as Lee prepared to meet Grant at
Appomattox Court House, one of his officers suggested
that, instead of surrendering, the army could melt into the
woods and carry on a guerrilla war. Lee rejected the idea.

*If I took your advice, the men . . . would be compelled
to rob and steal in order to live. They would become mere
bands of marauders. . . . We would bring on a state of
affairs it would take the country years to recover from.*

On April 20th, eleven days after he surrendered, Lee
tried to get Jefferson Davis to realize that continuing the
conflict would serve no useful purpose. He wrote:

*A partisan war may be continued, and hostilities pro-
tracted, causing individual suffering and the devastation of*

the country, but I see no prospect by that means of achieving a separate independence. . . . To save useless effusion of blood, I would recommend measures be taken for suspension of hostilities and the restoration of peace.

A D V I C E

When you have done all that you can and failed, don't drag out the inevitable. Waiting until after the organization's failure is public limits your options. Cut your losses, make the best deal you can, and move on. Lee wrote, "We failed, but in the good providence of God, apparent failure often proves a blessing."

After the war, in response to a question about why he looked sad, Lee said, "I'm thinking of the men who were lost after I knew it was too late."

A LASTING LEGACY

April 1865–October 1870

Lee does everything in his power to help the people of the South adjust to the post-Civil War realities. He sets the example by applying for a pardon and taking the oath of allegiance to the United States, and he encourages Southerners "to set manfully to work to restore the country, to rebuild their homes and churches, to educate their children." Although his preference is to quietly retire on a small farm, Lee, who believes that "the great duty of life is . . . the promotion of the happiness of our fellow men," accepts the presidency of Washington College "in the hope that I might be of some service to the country and the rising generation."

No one can have more at heart the welfare of the young men of the country than I have. . . . My only object is to endeavor to make them see their true interest, to teach them to labor diligently for their improvement, and to prepare themselves for the great work of life.

245. DON'T LOOK BACK

FROM THE MOMENT HE SURRENDERED, LEE TRIED NOT to look back. He wrote a friend, "I think it wisest not to keep open the sores of war." When asked to review a book about the war, Lee politely declined: "I have felt so little desire to recall the events of the war . . . that I have not read a single work that has been published on the subject."

Lee believed that it was "the duty of everyone to unite in the restoration of the country, and the reestablishment of peace and harmony." He advised General Jubal Early not to include, in a manuscript that Early was preparing, any "epithets or remarks calculated to excite bitterness or animosity between different sections of the country." Lee felt that "all controversy . . . will only serve to prolong angry and bitter feelings, and postpone the period when reason and charity may resume their sway." When malicious statements about him were brought to his attention, Lee chose not to reply.

I have thought from the time of the cessation of hostilities, that silence and patience on the part of the South was the true course, and I think so still. . . . These considerations have kept me from replying to accusations made against myself, and induced me to recommend the same to others.

ADVICE

There is no point in reopening old wounds. Being bitter about the past negatively impacts your ability to work effectively with others.

246. DEAL WITH HONORABLE PEOPLE

*O*N JUNE 7, 1865, A FEDERAL JUDGE HAD LEE INDICTED for treason. When Lee learned of the indictment, he wrote to Ulysses S. Grant:

I had supposed that officers and men of the Army of Northern Virginia were, by the terms of their surrender, protected by the United States Government from molestation so long as they conformed to its conditions. I am ready to meet any charges that may be preferred against me . . . but if I am correct as to the protection granted by my parole, and am not to be prosecuted, I desire to comply with the provisions of the President's proclamation, and therefore enclose the required application [for pardon].

Grant insisted that the proceedings against Lee be halted. He threatened to resign from the army, and make public his reasons for doing so, if they were not. On June 20th, Grant wrote to tell Lee that he would not be prosecuted and that he had forwarded Lee's request for a pardon "to the President, with the earnest recommendation that this application of General R. E. Lee for amnesty and pardon may be granted."

ADVICE

Doing business with companies that don't have a reputation for integrity is always a bad idea. Even the most carefully crafted accounting and legal mechanisms won't protect you from those who can't be trusted.

When Lee applied for a pardon, he was unaware that an oath of allegiance was required of former Confederate officers. On October 2, 1865, Lee signed the oath and sent it to Washington, but the U. S. Government never acknowledged its receipt. The oath was found in the National Archives 105 years later. In 1975, Congress granted Lee a pardon.

247. DO WHAT YOU CAN

AFTER RETURNING TO RICHMOND, BUT BEFORE ALL hostilities had ceased, a young soldier from a unit that had not yet surrendered asked Lee for advice. Lee told him, "Go home, all you boys who fought with me, and help to build up the shattered fortunes of our old state." On June 17, 1865, he wrote to Walter Taylor:

I am sorry to hear that our returned soldiers cannot obtain employment. Tell them they must all set to work, and, if they cannot do what they prefer, do what they can.

ADVICE

Losing your job or suffering some other business misfortune doesn't justify going off and sitting on the sidelines. Even if you can't do what you want, you still have an obligation to do what you can.

248. GIVE SOMETHING BACK

ON AUGUST 4, 1865, THE TRUSTEES OF WASHINGTON College in Lexington, Virginia met to review the school's financial condition and to select a new president. Lee had never been to Lexington, and he did not know any of the college's trustees. However, this did not deter them from deciding to offer him the presidency. The trustee who was chosen to deliver the offer to Lee had to borrow a suit since he had nothing presentable to wear, and the college borrowed $50 to cover his travel expenses.

In addition to the offer from the college, Lee received letters from two prominent Lexington residents urging him to accept the post. One wrote, "You can do a vast amount of good in building up this institution, and disseminating the blessings of education among our people." The other letter also stressed the importance of education, and it included this additional consideration: "While thus doing an important service . . . you might be presenting to the world . . . an example of quiet usefulness and gentle patriotism."

Lee went to discuss the offer with a friend, Reverend Joseph P. B. Wilmer. As Wilmer recalled:

The institution was one of local interest, and comparatively unknown to our people. I named others more conspicuous which would welcome him with ardor as their presiding head. I soon discovered that . . . in his judgment, the cause gave dignity to the institution and not the wealth of its endowment, or the renown of its scholars . . . and he only wished to be assured of his competency to fulfill the trust.

Lee, who had said that all he really wanted was to retire on a farm where he could have "fried chicken—not one fried chicken, or two, but unlimited fried chicken," accepted the position. On October 2, 1865, he took the oath of office as President of Washington College.

Lee's son, Rob, recalled that after his parents moved to Lexington, Lee received "an offer that he should be at the head of a large house to represent southern commerce . . . and have placed at his disposal an immense sum of money." Lee also received a number of other financially attractive job offers. He declined them all.

I have a self-imposed task which I must accomplish. I have led the young men of the South in battle; I have seen many of them die on the field; I shall devote my remaining energies to training young men to do their duty in life.

A D V I C E

Charles de Gaulle said, "Old age is a shipwreck." But it doesn't have to be. Jimmy Carter has shown that an ex-President can do more than write his memoirs and raise money for his Presidential Library. He can continue to serve his country. When the time comes for you to step down, plan on doing more than playing golf. Your knowledge, experience and wisdom are invaluable. You can help to educate the next generation or serve your community in other ways. You owe it to your country to give something back to help repay the opportunities you were afforded.

Three years later, the *New York Herald* suggested another job for Lee when it recommended that the Democratic Party nominate him to run against Grant for President in the election of 1868: "Let it nominate General R. E. Lee. . . . He is a better soldier than any of those they have thought upon and a greater man."

249. FIGUREHEAD

*I*F WASHINGTON COLLEGE'S TRUSTEES THOUGHT THAT Lee would be a figurehead president, they were in for a shock. As one professor recalled, "He [Lee] audited every account; he presided at every faculty meeting; studied and signed every report." Lee met with each student, and wrote their parents to tell them how they were doing in their studies. All of the activities at Washington College came under Lee's scrutiny and received his personal attention.

Lee believed that you had to earn your salary. When an insurance company offered to make him its president, at a salary of $10,000 a year, he declined, explaining that he had an obligation to Washington College. The insurance representative then told him that taking his company's presidency would not interfere with Lee's duties at the college. Lee did not understand how that was possible since being the President of Washington College was a full time job. The representative said, "We do not want you to discharge any duties. We simply wish the use of your name; that will abundantly compensate us." Lee was earning $1,500 a year at Washington College; the insurance company was offering him more than six times that amount simply for the use of his name. Lee replied, "I cannot consent to receive pay for services I do not render."

ADVICE

Many companies put retired senior executives on their boards. Sometimes all the company wants is to be able to note the presence of a respected individual on its board, and all the retired executive wants is the compensation and prestige that comes with the board seat. Nothing is more precious than your good name. Don't let money or prestige lure you into becoming a figurehead.

250. EXCUSES

ONE FORMER WASHINGTON COLLEGE STUDENT WROTE this account of his visit to Lee's office:

I was a frolicsome chap at college, and having been absent from class an unreasonable number of times, was finally summoned to the General's office. Abject terror took possession of me in the presence of such wise and quiet dignity; the reasons I had carefully prepared to give for my absence stood on their heads, or toppled over. In reply to General Lee's grave but perfectly polite question, I stammered out a story about a violent illness, and then, conscious that I was at that moment the picture of health, I hastened on with something about leaving my boots at the cobblers, when General Lee interrupted me: "Stop . . . stop, sir! One good reason is enough."

ADVICE

Some people can come up with creative excuses for not doing what they should. Be sure to differentiate between the valid reason for nonperformance and the carefully crafted excuse.

Lee always watched out for the students who weren't doing well. He told one new professor "to observe the stage driver's rule. . . . Always take care of the poor horses."

251. AN EXPANDING VISION

*P*RIOR TO LEE'S ASSUMING THE PRESIDENCY, THE students at Washington College had all taken the same classics-oriented curriculum. Lee set out to change that. He introduced the concept of electives, and within a month of his arrival, was proposing major new course offerings that included architecture, astronomy, chemistry, geology, metallurgy, physics, Spanish, and civil and mechanical engineering.

Lee did not formulate a vision for Washington College and then go about implementing it as if he were building a concrete structure. His was a dynamic and expanding vision. In March 1869, he proposed a school of business, a school of agriculture, a fellowship program for promising graduate students, a scholarship program for those wishing to study journalism, and a summer school program. All this was in addition to proposing new course offerings in academic disciplines, engineering studies, and vocational subjects such as photography.

According to Lee, "The great object of the whole plan is to provide the facilities required . . . by our young men, who, looking to an early entry into the practical pursuits of life, need a more direct training to this end than the usual literary courses." Lee was proposing that the college provide its students with a "practical education," but he was not suggesting that this be accomplished solely through technical and vocational courses. He went on to say, "The proposed departments will also derive great advantage from the literary [courses] . . . whose influence in the cultivation and enlargement of the mind is felt beyond their immediate limits." Technical training would take place within the framework of a liberal arts curriculum.

The *New York Herald* commented that, with his ideas about education, Lee was "likely to make as great an impression upon our fogy old schools and colleges as [he] did in military tactics upon our old fogy commanders in . . . the rebellion."

ADVICE

In today's rapidly changing world, organizations with a static vision will find it difficult to survive. Revisit your vision regularly to make sure it still encompasses all that you desire for your organization. A dynamic and expanding vision is a prerequisite to a healthy and vital enterprise.

$\mathcal{T}$HE MORNING AFTER HE TOOK OFFICE, LEE WROTE to his wife, "The scarcity of money everywhere embarrasses all proceedings." New physical facilities would have to be built and additional faculty hired to make Lee's vision for Washington College a reality. To raise money for the college, two local ministers conducted a mail solicitation campaign. Another traveled the country making personal appeals for "General Lee's College." Potential large donors were courted by Lee and the trustees.

On November 28, 1865, Lee wrote to Lexington's most illustrious son, Cyrus McCormick, the inventor of the reaper. He had never met McCormick, who had moved from Lexington to Chicago nearly twenty years earlier. Lee discussed the new curriculum that he wanted to implement. He was certain that McCormick would appreciate "the benefit of applying scientific knowledge and research to agriculture, mining, manufacturing." Lee did not ask McCormick for a contribution, but he did tell him that his former Lexington neighbors, "notwithstanding their impoverished condition," were doing all they could to raise the needed funds. "Their efforts, I am sure, will be strengthened by your sympathy; and your influence will cheer them in their meritorious work."

The rector of the college followed with a letter suggesting McCormick contribute the money for a new science building, to be named in his honor. "Can you come down with a good round sum to build up a school with which your name will be associated in all time to come?"

McCormick made an initial contribution of $10,000. Before the school year ended in June 1866, he had given another $5,000. During Lee's first year as President, Washington College took in over $100,000.

A D V I C E

Whether you are trying to raise money or get acceptance for a new idea, an effective approach is to begin with a soft sell that gently introduces the topic. Then, after you've given the party you're making the pitch to a little time to get used to the idea, follow up with a hard sell close. This one-two works best when the soft and hard sell arguments are presented by different individuals.

253. PUBLIC TESTIMONY

$\mathcal{T}$HE RADICAL REPUBLICAN MAJORITY IN CONGRESS
was opposed to President Andrew Johnson's conciliatory poli-
cies toward the South. They created a Joint Committee on
Reconstruction. On February 17, 1866, Lee testified before the
Committee. During the questioning, Lee was asked if "in the
event of a war between the United States and any foreign
power" the former Confederate States were given "a fair
prospect of gaining their independence and shaking off the government of the United States, is it, or is it not, your opinion that
they would avail themselves of the opportunity?" He replied:

*I cannot speak with certainty on that point. . . . I have
nothing whatever to base an opinion on. So far as I know,
they contemplate nothing of the kind now. What may happen
in the future I cannot say.*

In response to another hypothetical question, Lee said,
"I cannot pretend to foresee events."

A D V I C E

When making public statements, whether testifying in a legal
proceeding, appearing before a governmental body, or giving
an interview, there are no substitutes for accuracy and brevity.
If you don't know the answer to a question, say so. If it's a fac-
tual question, saying, "I don't know" is better than giving a
wrong answer. If you are asked a hypothetical question, saying,
"I cannot predict the future" is both an honest and a safe
answer. Any speculation on your part is subject to deliberate
distortion or to being taken out of context and misinterpreted.

Lee did testify that the Civil War "was brought about by the politicians of the
country. . . . I did believe at the time that it was an unnecessary condition of affairs
and might have been avoided, if forbearance and wisdom had been practiced on
both sides."

254. TRUST

*I*N THE FALL OF 1866, SEVERAL STUDENTS REALIZED THAT someone was stealing their firewood. To catch the culprit, they drilled a hole in a log, filled it with gunpowder, and replaced it on their woodpile. Early the next morning, the stove in one of the professor's rooms exploded. Fortunately, the flying metal fragments did not injure any-one. The professor was convinced that someone had tried to murder him. Who did it was a mystery until later that morning when two students came to Lee and told him what they had done. After they had finished, Lee laughed and said:

Your plan to find out who was taking your wood was a good one, but your powder charge was too heavy. Next time use less powder.

ADVICE

Your people pay you the greatest compliment when they voluntarily tell you something that you were unlikely to find out for yourself. There is no one thing you can do to achieve this level of trust. It is built upon words and deeds over time.

*I*N 1865, THE STUDENTS AT WASHINGTON COLLEGE HAD enjoyed a one-week Christmas break. In 1866, Lee announced that he was going to follow the example of the University of Virginia and eliminate the Christmas vacation. Only Christmas Day would be a holiday. After a student petition to reinstate the Christmas vacation was denied, student leaders began circulating a pledge not to attend classes during the period from Christmas through New Year's Day. They quickly had seventy signatures, and it seemed that every student would sign it. Lee walked over to the bulletin board where the pledge was posted and said:

Every man that signs that paper will be summarily dismissed. If all sign it, I shall lock up the college and put the keys in my pocket.

ADVICE

If you allow yourself to be bullied into one concession, you will be forced to make others. Once the process of giving in to threats begins, there is no stopping. The best way to meet a threat is head-on. However, for counter-threats to be effective, they must be perceived as credible. This requires a reputation for matching words with actions, not for talking tough and then backing off.

256. UNENFORCEABLE RULES

*L*EE REGULARLY ADMONISHED THE FACULTY TO "NEVER make a rule that we cannot enforce." When asked by a new student for a copy of the school's rules, Lee replied, "We have only one rule here—to act like a gentleman at all times." In the catalogue for the 1867–1868 academic year, Lee introduced an honor code.

The discipline has been placed upon that basis on which . . . experience has shown it can be most safely trusted—upon the honor and self-respect of the students themselves.

A D V I C E

An unenforceable rule is worse than having no rule because it implicitly sanctions bad behavior.

Lee believed that "you should not force young men to do their duty, but let them do it voluntarily and thereby develop their characters." Before Lee became President of Washington College, the students had been required to attend a daily morning prayer service in the college chapel. Lee attended services every morning, but he eliminated the requirement for the students to attend.

257. DISRESPECT

*L*EE TOLD ONE STUDENT WHO WAS DOING POORLY, "If you do not improve, you will fail your work." When the student replied, "But General, you were a failure," Lee said, "Yes, but let us hope you will be more fortunate than I."

On another occasion, Lee told a student who had been called to his office:

Chewing is particularly obnoxious to me. Go out and remove that quid, and never appear before me again chewing tobacco.

The next time the student came to Lee's office, he was again chewing tobacco. Lee wrote a brief note and handed it to him. The student read that he had been "dismissed from Washington College for disrespect to the President."

ADVICE

There is a fine line between being brash and being disrespectful. Tolerate the former, but not the latter.

258. RECONCILIATION

ULYSSES S. GRANT WAS INAUGURATED AS THE EIGHTEENTH President of the United States on March 4, 1869. One of his first steps as President was to invite Lee to the White House. Lee accepted, and they met on May 1st. What Grant and Lee talked about was not as important as the fact that they met in the White House. Lee personified the South. In inviting him, Grant had made a gesture of reconciliation. By accepting Grant's invitation, Lee had reciprocated in kind.

Since the end of the war, Lee had been urging reconciliation. When he took the oath of allegiance to the United States, he explained to one of his sons that it was right of him to set the example. To General Beauregard, he wrote:

True patriotism sometimes requires of men to act exactly contrary, at one period, to that which it does at another, and the motive which impels them—the desire to do right—is precisely the same. The circumstances which govern their actions change, and their conduct must conform to the new order of things.

Grant recognized that the people of the South would "be guided to a great extent by his [Lee's] example." In this he was correct. When one young man told his father, a former Confederate general, that he had taken the oath, he was told, "You have disgraced the family!" His reply, "General Lee advised me to do it," drew this response: "Oh, that alters the case. Whatever General Lee says is all right."

ADVICE

After a merger or acquisition, particularly if it was a hostile takeover, seek out opportunities to make gestures of friendship and reconciliation.

Lee wrote a friend that the people of the South should "qualify themselves to vote, and elect . . . wise and patriotic men, who will devote their abilities to the interests of the country, and the healing of all dissensions. I have invariably recommended this course since the cessation of all hostilities, and have endeavored to practice it myself." When in 1867, it was suggested he become Governor of Virginia, Lee declined on the grounds that his election might "excite hostility toward the State . . . and I, therefore, cannot consent to become the instrument of bringing distress upon those whose prosperity and happiness are so dear to me."

259. DISPARAGING REMARKS

*W*HEN LEE HEARD A PROFESSOR AT WASHINGTON College making disparaging remarks about Ulysses S. Grant, he said to the man:

Sir, if you ever again presume to speak disrespectfully of General Grant in my presence, either you or I will sever his connection with this university.

ADVICE

You lower yourself to the level of a guttersnipe by making nasty comments about someone else, and you show yourself to be a weak manager when you let your staff do it.

260. A LASTING LEGACY

$\mathcal{R}$OBERT E. LEE DIED ON OCTOBER 12, 1870. HE LEFT a lasting legacy. Lee is best remembered as a brilliant general and that memory is honored at West Point. Cadets are housed in a building named for him, and they study the strategy and tactics that won him fame on the battlefield.

Less than a month after he had surrendered his army at Appomattox, the *New York Herald* reported Lee's promise "to make any sacrifice or perform any honorable act that would tend to the restoration of peace." An important part of Lee's legacy was the way he kept that promise. After the Civil War, he set an example that helped to bind the nation's wounds. Lee's postwar contribution to peace was summed up by one of his former staff officers: "He set to work to use his great influence to reconcile the people of the South to the hard consequences of their defeat, to inspire them with hope, to lead them to accept, freely and frankly, the government that had been established by the result of the war."

Two months before he died, Lee called a meeting of the Washington College Board of Trustees. He wanted to raise $100,000 for an astronomical observatory. Five years earlier the trustees had borrowed $50 to pay the travel expenses of the man who was carrying their offer of the presidency to Lee. When he had taken office the school was, in the words of one of the trustees, "a broken down college." Lee's goal had been to raise Washington College "to a level with the best institutions in the country." He had done that and more. He had established the model for the modern American University, and he had done it under the most adverse circumstances. After Lee died, the trustees petitioned the Virginia Legislature for permission to change the school's name to Washington and Lee University. They were not paying tribute to the general or the conciliator. They were honoring one of America's foremost educators.

A D V I C E

Robert E. Lee led armies in battle, helped reconcile a people to their defeat, and built a great educational institution. Lee never worried about his legacy; he focused on the job at hand. He believed that our legacy is the work we do to improve the human condition and bring about better times: "We may not see them but our children will, and we will live over again in them."

Of Lee's passing, Jefferson Davis said, "When the monument we build shall have crumbled into dust, his virtues will still live, a high model for the imitation of generations yet unborn."

Human nature will not change. In any future great national trial, compared with the men of this, we shall have as weak and as strong, as silly and as wise, as bad and as good. Let us therefore study the incidents of this, as philosophy to learn wisdom from.

—Abraham Lincoln

INDEX